MW00815367

COMPLIMENTS OF . . .

Global Imports

770-951-BMWS
ATLANTA

THE WORLD OF
GOLF

THE WORLD OF
GOLF

ANTONY ATHA

SMITHMARK

© Anness Publishing Limited 1997

All rights reserved. No part of this publication may be
reproduced, stored in a retrieval system, or transmitted in any
way or by any means, electronic, mechanical, photocopying,
recording or otherwise, without the prior written permission
of the copyright holder.

This edition published in 1997 by
Smithmark Publishers, a division of U.S. Media Holdings Inc.,
16 East 32nd Street, New York, NY 10016.

Smithmark books are available for bulk purchase for sales promotion
and for premium use. For details write or call the manager of special sales,
Smithmark Publishers, 16 East 32nd Street, New York, NY 10016;
(212) 532-6600

ISBN 0-7651-9420-1

Produced by Anness Publishing Limited
Hermes House
88-89 Blackfriars Road
London SE1 8HA

Printed in Singapore by
Star Standard Industries Pte Ltd

10 9 8 7 6 5 4 3 2 1

**Page 1: A woman golfer gracing the
front cover of the *Chicago Tribune*,
1922.**
**Page 2: "The Golfers: A Grand Match
Played Over St Andrews Links", from
a painting by Charles Lees, 1841.**
**Page 3: Golfers playing at St Andrews
in 1933, from a poster for London and
North Eastern Railway.**
**Pages 4-5: A line-up of leading
professionals c.1904, Harry Vardon,
Ben Sayers, Willie Auchterlonie,
Andrew Kirkaldy and Willie Fernie.**

CONTENTS

●●●●●●●●●●●●●●●●●●●●●●●●●●●●

6 **Introduction**

Chapter 1
9 **Origins and History**

Chapter 2
37 **Famous Golfers**

Chapter 3
51 **The Great Tournaments**

Chapter 4
67 **The Great Courses**

Chapter 5
93 **Collectables and Memorabilia**

96 **Index**

INTRODUCTION

• •

Golf is played in almost every country in the world and has a huge following. The major tournaments are followed avidly by large crowds and millions more watch on television; the finest players are fêted and applauded, and the ordinary golfer marvels at the supreme skill that they show.

For all players – amateur, professional, novice and holiday hacker – the beauty of golf lies in the search for perfection which is ultimately unattainable. Yet the Goddess of Fortune gives brief glimpses of this Nirvana. All golfers will have struck one perfect shot, long etched in the memory, where the ball soars straight towards the distant flag or bounces twice on the green before running into the hole. At that moment the veriest amateur is on level terms with Nick Faldo or Severiano Ballesteros.

The other great advantage that golf has over all other games is the handicapping system which allows competitive matches to be played between players of vastly differing abilities, and for women to play on equal terms with men. This is golf's greatest asset.

Golf has a long history and the origins are lost in the past. No-one will ever be able to say for certain where golf started and who struck the first shot. The theories of the origins of the game are many and the history of golf is outlined briefly in the first chapter of this book. Later chapters cover a number of the great courses in the world, the tournaments and the great players. There can be little argument over any list of the really great players. People may quibble over a list of the very good players, whom to put in and whom to leave out, but the really great players have all won a number of the world's major championships. Their achievements speak for themselves.

Any selection of the world's great courses in a book of this size is invidious and there are many courses worthy of inclusion which have been omitted. Lack of space is the culprit.

Golf courses are often situated in beautiful surroundings; Augusta, Cypress Point, Portmarnock. But for many golfers the finest are the links courses of Scotland where golf began. There the grass is short and springy, the rough unplayable and the sea winds sweep in over the dunes. That is golf at its best.

Antony Atha

Above: The first Open champions.

Right: A stymie, from an old advertisement. Stymies were abolished in 1951.

CHAPTER 1

ORIGINS AND HISTORY

● ● ● ● ● ● ● ● ● ● ● ● ● ● ● ● ● ● ● ●

The origins of golf are lost in the mists of time, and the first few hundred years of its history are uncertain, but the steady rise in its popularity from the 1700s onwards is indisputable.

Right: A well-dressed and rather dashing golfer from the cover of *Harper's Magazine*, April 1898.

Opposite: A portrait of Harold Hilton, Open, British Amateur and American Amateur champion. He was the first editor of *Golfing Monthly*.

THE ORIGINS OF GOLF

Right: Japanese courtesans while away the time playing a form of indoor golf.

Below: An illustration taken from a medieval manuscript showing what could be either golf or a form of hockey.

"It answers to a simple rustic pastime of the Romans in which they played with a ball of leather stuffed with feathers, called *Paganica*, and the golf-ball is composed of the same materials to this day. In the reign of Edward the Third (AD 1327–77) the Latin name, *Cambuca*, was applied to this pastime, and it derived the denomination, no doubt, from the crooked club or bat with which it was played."

Joseph Strutt (1749–1803),
Sports and Pastimes of the People of England

There is heated debate over where golf was invented, when it first came to be played and how it was first played. Some claim that the game originated in England, and they point to the Crécy window in Gloucester Cathedral which shows a faceless golfer swinging a club, as if playing a short approach shot. The window was designed and built between 1340 and 1350 and it is certainly the earliest pictorial record of such an activity. Other researches have discovered illustrations of Japanese ladies playing a game indoors with clubs, and there have been claims from Italy and France.

Above: An illustration taken from a fourteenth-century illuminated Book of Prayer. The two men are playing some form of game with ball and clubs which could well be an early game of golf.

The main claims come from Holland and Scotland. The Dutch historian van Hengel has claimed that golf started in Holland, where it originated from a game called *spel metten kolve*. This was later shortened to *het kolve* and then *kolf*. This game was first played on a four-hole course, each hole measuring a thousand yards, to commemorate the relief of Kronenburg Castle in 1297. The "holes" were on doors, a windmill, a kitchen, an outhouse and the castle itself. There is ample evidence that a game of this type was played frequently in Holland, on the ice in winter, in the towns (where it was banned because of the damage caused by the participants) and in the countryside. Van Hengel's theory is that *kolf* was played by the Dutch seamen who brought their clubs with them to Leith when they traded with Scotland during the fourteenth century. They were the people who introduced the game to Scotland and this theory is supported by the large numbers of "featheries", the first golf balls made of leather stuffed with boiled feathers, which were exported from Holland to Scotland during the sixteenth century. While it is true that there may be a link between "golfe" as played

in Scotland and "kolf" as played in Holland, there are as many differences as there are similarities. The Dutch golfers were still hitting balls at posts three centuries after Scottish golfers were hitting their balls into holes and most people prefer to believe that golf started in Scotland on the stretch of land on the south coast of the Firth of Forth from Leith to Dunbar. The written evidence to support this claim is sparse. There is a record of a golf ball being sold for ten Scottish shillings in 1452 and on 6th March 1457 came the first hard evidence that golf was frequently played in Scotland when it was banned by decree in the Fourteenth Parliament of King James II: "And that the fute-bal and golfe be utterly cryed downe, and not to be used." The decree was repeated in 1491 in the reign of King James IV when it was declared that "It is statute and ordained that in na place of the Realme there be usyt Fute-baw, Golfe, or other sik unprofitable sportis contrary to the good of the Realme and defense thereof." Football and golf were interfering with the archery practice necessary to defend the country from invasion by England, although for how long either

Holland's claim to be the country which invented golf is based on paintings like this which show "kolf" being played on the ice with skaters in a landscape.

An early golfer.

Shinty, a free-for-all form of hockey, had the same appeal – of hitting a ball with a stick – as golf.

James V, had played the game in France when she was married to the dauphin Francis, and had had her clubs carried by young cadets, which is probably where the name and occupation of caddies came from. She was charged with being seen playing golf and pall-mall in the field beside Seton, shortly after the murder of her husband Lord Darnley in 1567.

The most attractive theory of the origin of the game was put forward in 1886 by Sir Walter Simpson. He claimed that a shepherd was looking after his flock of sheep grazing on the links, that part of the coast lying behind the sand dunes, when one day he started hitting small pebbles with his crook and saw one of them disappear down a rabbit hole. He was able to repeat this shot and the other shepherds followed his example, and so the game of golf was born. Fanciful or not, it is possible that there is some truth in this story. There is an instinctive pleasure in hitting stones and balls with sticks. The shepherd's crook developed into a club, the feathery ball came into use as being more reliable and less hard than a pebble or solid wooden ball. Golf gradually evolved.

By the middle of the fifteenth century, golf had spread rapidly throughout Scotland. The

sport had been played and by how many people will probably always remain a mystery.

Ten years later King James IV had taken up the game himself. There are records in the accounts of the Lord High Treasurer of the purchase of clubs in 1502, and also of a match played between the King and the Earl of Bothwell in 1504. Intermarriage between royal families spread the game to England and France. Mary, Queen of Scots, daughter of

An artist's impression of Mary Queen of Scots, carrying a golf club. While she was in France her clubs were carried by cadets, the origin of the word caddies.

first courses were at Leith, on the Firth of Forth just outside Edinburgh, and Bruntsfield in the centre of the city. Other courses recorded in the sixteenth century include St Andrews, Perth, Montrose, Dornoch, Banff, North Inch and Aberdeen. Along with football, it became the national game. When James VI, the son of Mary, Queen of Scots, became king of England in 1603 as James I, he and his courtiers started playing at Blackheath, just outside London, which became the first golf course in England. The Royal Blackheath Golf Club, though not founded until 1766, became the first English golf club.

The length of the early golf courses varied enormously and there was a great difference between churchyard courses and the links courses. It was a time when attendance at church was compulsory on Sundays and churchgoing was combined with archery practice. People met and played games and when golf was banned on the links, courses were set up within the churchyards. Each hole measured 50–100 yards (45–90m) and the ball was hit at a target with one club.

This practice was, initially, condoned by the church authorities except at the time of the sermon, but as religious attitudes of the church hardened towards the end of the sixteenth century, the playing of golf was prohibited on Sundays. There is a record at the Kirk Session of North Leith that on 11th February, 1608, "John Henrie, Pat. Bogie, James Kid, George Robertsoune and James Watsoune, being accusit for playing of the gowff everie Sabboth the tyme of the sermonnes, notwithstanding oft admonitioun past befoir, were convict[ed] ilk ane of them, and ordainit to be wardet [put in prison] until the same were payit."

Links courses were of varying lengths and numbers of holes. The original course at Leith had five holes measuring 414, 461, 426, 495 and 435 yards (378, 420, 389, 452 and 398m), which must have taken a considerable number of strokes with long-nosed clubs and feathery balls: Blackheath originally had seven holes, while St Andrews had 22, 11 holes out and 11 back. In 1764 William St Clair played the 22 holes in 121 strokes, and as a result the first four holes were reduced to two to make

the average scoring higher. As the same holes were played out and back, the course then became 18 holes and subsequently this became the standard number for all courses. Generally, the courses marched out in a straight line and then back with the same holes being played in both directions.

However, as courses became more crowded the fairways were expanded although this is the origin of the famous double greens seen on the Old Course at St Andrews in Scotland to this day.

As golf became more popular it also became more exclusive. From 1735 onwards

King Charles I of England receives news of the rebellion in Ireland whilst playing golf on Leith links.

The 7th and 11th on the Old Course, St Andrews.

Above: Members of the Honourable Company of Edinburgh Golfers carry the club and balls of office in procession.

groups of friends started to form clubs. The Royal Burgess Society of Edinburgh was the first in that year, followed by the Honourable Company of Edinburgh Golfers in 1744 and the Royal and Ancient Golf Club of St Andrews in 1754. In the same year as the Honourable Company of Edinburgh Golfers was founded, they petitioned the Edinburgh City Council to present a prize for which they would compete. The prize was a silver golf club and the first-ever official golf competition was won by a famous Edinburgh surgeon, John Rattray. Rattray had attended the wounded after the Battle of Prestonpans in the 1745 rebellion and was later captured at the Battle of Culloden.

Rules were drawn up for the competition and the Leith Code with 13 rules was adopted the following year by the Royal and Ancient Golf Club of St Andrews. The majority of these are unchanged and even today they are the most important rules of golf, which now extend to over 40 pages. The main rules were: VII, which directed the player to play for the hole and not his opponent's ball when holing out on the green; V, which said that balls could be lifted from any hazard and played, allowing a one stroke penalty; IX, which prohibited the player from marking the way to the

Right: A mid-eighteenth-century Edinburgh golfer who looks more likely to miss the ball than hit it.

VI ET ARTE

hole when on the green; and XII, which instructed the player furthest from the hole to play first. All these rules still apply.

From these beginnings golf evolved over the next hundred years. There was a period, however, at the end of the eighteenth and beginning of the nineteenth century when the game fell into disrepute, membership declined and many of the original clubs in Scotland ceased to exist. Even St Andrews had to take a legal dispute to the House of Lords to establish their right to play golf on the Old Course which was, at that time, threatened by a rabbit-breeding business. It is difficult to say exactly why this happened: possibly the influence of the French Revolution made people alive to the difference between rich and poor as never before. Golf as a game previously played by all classes was becoming the preserve of the gentry, which made it unpopular. The disastrous rebellion of 1745-6 in Scotland may have had an effect as many of the aristocracy either went into exile or moved to London and the south in its aftermath. Generally, the Napoleonic Wars were a period of high inflation, there was increased demand for food, courses were ploughed up for wheat or built over as people were drawn into towns in the wake of the Industrial Revolution. Inflation hit the finances of many courses. Whatever the cause, this hiccup was only temporary. By 1850 golf was re-established, it had regained its place in Scottish society as the premier national pastime and from there it spread to England and Europe and overseas as the Scots emigrated all over the globe.

William Innes, the Blackheath golfer, painted by L.F. Abbott.

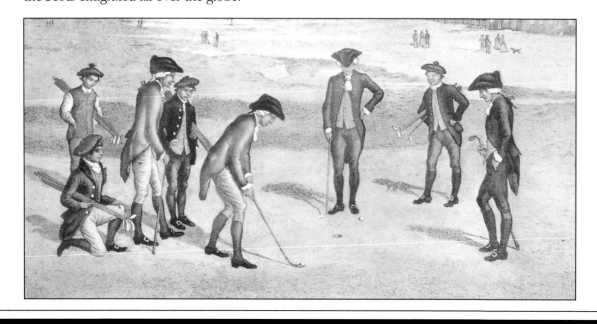

The first green at St Andrews, from an engraving by Frank Paton dated 1798.

THE END OF THE NINETEENTH CENTURY

Golf exposes every facet of the human character. Admiral Maitland Dougall was to play in the Club Medal at St Andrews in 1860. The day was one of vile weather with violent rain and gales. A vessel was in trouble in the bay and the lifeboat was launched to rescue the crew. The Admiral took the stroke oar and the lifeboat was at sea for five hours. When it returned he went on to the tee to play his round and he won the medal, going round the course in just 112 strokes. He had bored a hole in his ball and filled it with buckshot to weigh it down and keep it low in the wind.

The second half of the nineteenth century saw the expansion of golf throughout the British Isles and from there to the further flung outposts of the British Empire and, finally, rather later in the day, to the USA. The expansion of golf was fuelled by a number of things: the advent of the guttie ball, which was not only cheaper but available in thousands rather than hundreds; the availability of mass-produced clubs; and the advent of the railways, which enabled people to travel easily. As travel became easier, the idea of holidays away from home took hold. Many of the seaside resorts built golf courses to attract the summer visitors, imitating the older courses of the resorts of North Berwick and Dunbar on the Firth of Forth.

The explosion of golf's popularity when it came was dramatic. In 1850 there were 24 clubs in Great Britain, by 1900 there were over 1,200. The first English seaside links course was Westward Ho! in north Devon, which was designed by "Old" Tom Morris in 1864. This was the home course of J. H. Taylor, one of the three greatest English golfers of all time. Other courses soon followed, particularly around the south-east coast of England. Royal St George's in the county of Kent was founded in 1887, its sister course Prince's in 1904. Aldeburgh and Southwold in Suffolk were both founded in 1884, two years after Great Yarmouth, just up the coast. In Lancashire, the Royal Liverpool, one of the oldest clubs in the country, was founded in 1869 and Haydock Park in 1877, while the championship links of Royal Birkdale and Royal Lytham and St Annes were founded in 1889 and 1886 respectively.

Above: Golf on Wimbledon Common, c.1890.

Below: Golfers playing at Pau in France, 1887.

The Scottish professional golfers at the Leith Open Tournament, 1867.

As holiday-makers, the British also started the game in Europe. The first club on the continent was founded at Pau in France, in the shadow of the Pyrenees, in 1856 and the Royal Antwerp Club in Belgium dates from 1888. When it moved in 1910 to Kepellenbos the club employed Willie Park Jnr as architect to lay out their new course.

Golf also spread abroad as the Scots emigrated throughout the British Empire. Unsurprisingly, the first overseas clubs were in India: the Royal Calcutta Club was founded in 1829 and the Royal Bombay Club in 1842. The Royal Christchurch Club in New Zealand was founded in 1867 and the Otago Club in 1871. Golf is thought to have been played in Australia by 1870 but, in fact, the first club, the Royal Melbourne, was not founded until 1891, with the Royal Adelaide and Royal Sydney Clubs following in 1892 and 1893 respectively. There was a golf club in Mauritius in 1844 and the Royal Hong Kong Club was founded in 1889. Inevitably, golf had started in Canada, a country with many connections with Scotland. The Royal Montreal Club was founded in 1873 and the Royal Quebec Club two years later. In South Africa, the Royal Cape Club was founded in 1885.

The Sea Hole, from an engraving dated 1889.

Members of the Royal and
Ancient Club, St Andrews,
Scotland c.1854.

North Berwick, c.1890.
The Berwick Law is on
the right with the harbour
in the background.

It is perhaps surprising that golf arrived rather late in the country that has since produced the finest players the world has ever seen, the USA. In fact, the first games of golf in the USA were played during the American War of Independence in the south, around Charleston in South Carolina. The South Carolina Golf Club was formed in 1786 and a Savannah Golf Club existed ten years later. However, this initial enthusiasm was short-lived and the game soon disappeared.

In 1887 Robert Lockhart, an expatriate Scot from Dunfermline, paid a visit to St Andrews. He ordered six golf clubs and two dozen gutta-percha balls, or gutties, from "Old" Tom Morris for his friend John Reid, who was an iron founder in Yonkers, New York, and is credited with being the father of modern American golf. The clubs and balls were forwarded and Lockhart, who had played golf as a boy in Scotland, tried them out on a meadow near the Hudson River in the autumn of 1887 before handing them over to Reid. He was the first person to hit a golf ball on American soil for nearly one hundred years. The following spring, Reid and five of his friends laid out the first three-hole course and later a six-hole course when they moved to a larger plot of land between North Broadway and Shonnard Place. On 14th November 1888, Reid proposed that they form a society to be called the St Andrews' Golf Club of Yonkers, in honour of St Andrews, the home of golf and the place where their first clubs had come from. In 1892 they moved to a

34-acre apple orchard in Weston and they have become known as "The Apple Tree Gang" from their habit of sitting under the apple trees when they had finished their game.

Reid's example spread rapidly through the USA and clubs were founded in Kentucky, Chicago, Shinnecock Hills, Brookline, Southampton and Newport, Rhode Island. In 1894 Theodore Havemeyer was elected the first president of the USGA. In 1895 two tournaments were held at Newport, the United States Amateur Championship and the United States Open Championship. By the turn of the century there were over 1,000 clubs in America. Golf in the USA was on its way and it did not take the first champions long to appear.

Golf arrives in America. *The Apple Tree Gang* **from a painting by Leland Gustavson.**

The construction crew for a new American golf course line up for a photo opportunity, c.1910.

EQUIPMENT

The development of the golf ball from wood – at the bottom of the picture – to feathery, to the gutta-percha ball, or guttie, and finally – at the top – the rubber-core ball invented by Coburn Haskell.

Golf is an easy game to comprehend and for all players, amateur, professional, hack handicapper or beginner, there is the supreme thrill of that one perfectly struck shot which soars over the intervening bunkers and settles within two feet of the hole. This opinion of golf is not universal. Mark Twain referred to golf as a way of spoiling a good walk; someone else said that it was a futile game: "hitting little balls with little sticks into little holes".

It is worth pausing at this point to look in detail at the equipment used in the game of golf. As it improved and changed so did the game and the rise in popularity of golf at the end of the nineteenth century can largely be attributed to the introduction of new materials and the impact of mass production.

The first really important item of equipment in the first two hundred or more years of the game was the golf ball, or "feathery", which replaced the first primitive balls made from iron, wood and lead. The feathery was made from three pieces of hide stitched together with waxed twine, turned inside out and then stuffed with boiled goose feathers which were inserted with the help of a long iron brogue with a wooden cross handle, which the ballmaker used to press against his chest to exert more pressure. When the ball was roughly round, the last stitches were put in and it was knocked into final shape with a heavy hammer and left to dry. After two days the feathers expanded and the leather contracted, and the result was a hard round ball which was rubbed with oil to make it waterproof and chalk to make it more visible. Featheries were expensive to make and were sold for two shillings and sixpence each, with the finest being made by the Gourlays of Musselburgh and priced at four to five shillings. For many years at the beginning of the nineteenth century, it was fashionable to play with a Gourlay ball. But the output remained small and the price high, and they disappeared almost overnight when the gutta-percha, or "guttie", ball appeared in 1848.

The guttie was invented by a St Andrews clergyman, Robert Adam Paterson, who received a statue of Vishnu from India which had been packed in gutta-percha for safety. He discovered that gutta could be cut into pieces, softened in boiling water and then rolled into a ball which hardened as it cooled. He promptly took out a patent and sold the manufacturing rights to a London firm. Balls made of gutta-percha cost about a quarter the price of a feathery golf ball and they became the first mass-produced golfing item. The demise of the feathery and rise of the guttie helped to spread the popularity of golf throughout the world. There were problems with the original guttie balls as at the time aerodynamics was but imperfectly understood. It became apparent that they flew much better when they became scratched and scuffed, and it then became the practice to hammer markings on to the ball before they were sold.

Above left: A guttie ball.

Above right: The mould for a guttie ball. The arrival of the guttie did much to make golf a popular sport.

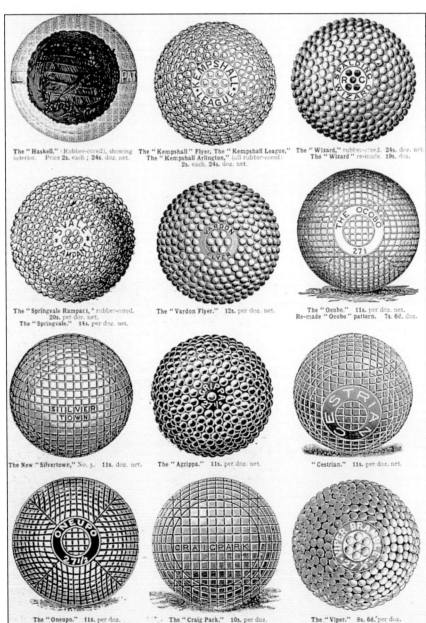

The "Haskell." (Rubber-cored), showing interior. Price 2s. each ; 24s. doz. net.

The "Kempshall" Flyer, The "Kempshall League," The "Kempshall Arlington," (all rubber-cored) 2s. each. 24s. doz. net.

The "Wizard," rubber-cored. 24s. doz. net. The "Wizard" re-made. 19s. doz.

The "Springvale Rampart," rubber-cored. 20s. per doz. net. The "Springvale." 14s. per doz. net.

The "Vardon Flyer." 12s. per doz. net.

The "Ocobo." 11s. per doz. net. Re-made "Ocobo" pattern. 7s. 6d. doz.

The New "Silvertown," No. 5. 11s. doz. net.

The "Agrippa." 11s. per doz. net.

"Cestrian." 11s. per doz. net.

The "Oneupo." 11s. per doz. Re-made, "St. Mungo." 7s. 6d. per doz.

The "Craig Park." 10s. per doz.

The "Viper." 8s. 6d. per doz.

Above: Golf balls at the end of the nineteenth century. Featheries are on the left and gutties on the right.

UNDERSTUDIES

Above: "Understudies", from the Badminton Library volume on *Golf* published in 1890.

Left: An advertisement for well-seasoned rubber-cored balls. The indentation patterns are striking and various.

Above left: An early nineteenth-century long-nosed wood.

Above middle: A wood made by Hugh Philp c.1850.

Above right: A blacksmith's iron, c.1790.

Right: Robert Forgan's workshop at St Andrews c.1890, with Forgan seated on the left. He started the mass-production of golf clubs and introduced the hickory shaft.

The introduction of mass-produced guttie balls radically changed the type and design of the golf club. The first golf clubs, long-nosed woods, were made from a variety of woods, often fruit wood inlaid with ram's horn. It was a skilled individual craft and clubmakers such as William Mayne, Simon Cossar and Hugh Philp were much sought after as suppliers of the finest equipment. But the advent of the guttie changed the shape of the golf club because a guttie ball was much harder than a feathery. No longer was it necessary, or possible, to sweep the feathery off the turf with a long flat swing, and the delicate, long-nosed clubs made by Hugh Philp began to split when they were used with the harder guttie balls. To counteract this, the head was redesigned. It became shorter and broader, more like a modern wood, and the new clubs were known as "bulgers". A few years later, iron clubs became increasingly popular as the guttie withstood the impact of an iron in a way that a feathery never could. Irons could be made in forges and so mass-produced just like the guttie. Robert Forgan, a nephew of Hugh Philp, took over his clubmaking business and started the mass-production of golf clubs. He introduced the hickory shaft which was used in the best clubs for many years, but by the turn of the century, clubmakers were experimenting with steel shafts. The first steel-shafted clubs were made in Britain in 1912. They were widely used in the USA by the 1920s but were banned by the Royal and Ancient until 1929 when the Prince of Wales used a set at St Andrews. Many of the leading professionals of the day started using steel-shafted clubs as they found them more consistent than those made with hickory.

Golf clubs have continued to evolve over the last 70 years and new materials like carbon, titanium and boron have made clubs lighter and stronger so that the ball can be hit even further. The "Big Bertha" range of drivers is the latest introduction. The basic shape of a golf club has changed little since the end of the nineteenth century.

The last major change was the introduction of the Haskell rubber-cored ball in 1901, which did to the guttie what the guttie had

A drawing of a set of modern golf clubs in 1890: seven woods, three irons and a putting cleek.

done to the feathery. The Haskell ball flew much further and gave the professionals much more control over their shots. It increased the popularity of the game tenfold. Modern balls may have improved in aerodynamic design but essentially the rubber-cored ball has remained the same for the last 95 years.

Increased distance brought about by improvements in equipment has a long and honourable history in golf. The arrival of the Haskell ball transformed the game at the turn of the century.

HASKELL ROYAL 2/- EACH

OF ALL DEALERS AND PROFESSIONALS OR FROM THE SOLE MANUFACTURERS
THE B.F. GOODRICH Co.
7, SNOW HILL, LONDON, E.C.
A sample ball sent post free on receipt of P.O. value 2/- from the manufacturers.

"I must have his name & address – he's driven beyond the limit."

1890–1945

The first competitions in the 1860s were small affairs dominated by the professional golfers of Scotland. Professionals were not generally held in very high regard. They occupied a no-man's land, part teacher, part clubmaker and mender, ball-maker and part greenkeeper. In the twentieth century this changed and, as the game of golf took hold of the collective imagination of each nation, they became heroes, fêted in the press, with increasingly greater financial rewards open to them. At the turn of the twentieth century the golfing world was dominated by the "Great Triumvirate" from Great Britain of J. H. Taylor, Harry Vardon and James Braid. After World War I the domination of the game crossed the Atlantic, and many would claim it has stayed there ever since.

Apart from the "Great Triumvirate", there were a number of outstanding players on both sides of the Atlantic. John Ball from Liverpool was one of the most successful amateur players of all time, winning the British Amateur Championship no fewer than eight times between 1888 and 1912. He also became the first amateur and the first Englishman to win the Open when he won at Prestwick in 1890. Ball's main rival as an amateur was Harold H. Hilton who, like Ball, came from Liverpool.

Hilton won the Amateur Championship four times; he won the Open twice in 1892 and 1897, when he beat James Braid into second place. Hilton then went to the USA and his tour was dubbed "Childe Harold's Pilgrimage". In 1911 he beat Fred Herreshoff at the 37th hole to become the only British winner of the US Amateur Championship in the history of the event.

Top right: The "Great Triumvirate" of Vardon, Braid and Taylor won the Open Championship sixteen times between them between 1894 and 1914.

Bottom left: Harold Hilton was British and American Amateur Champion in 1911. He also won the Open twice.

Bottom right: John Ball was British Amateur Champion a record eight times between 1888 and 1912.

24.—HAROLD HILTON.

25.—J. BALL.
A Celebrated Golf Ball.

The first US Amateur Champion was the redoubtable Charles Blair Macdonald who had such an immense influence on the evolution of golf in the USA. He was followed by two great amateurs, Walter Travis and Jerome Travers.

Travis won the US Amateur Championship in 1900, 1901 and 1903, and the British Championship in 1904. This was a great achievement and a breakthrough for the sport in the USA as it was the first time an American had won any title in Britain. Travers won his first US Amateur title in 1907 and then again in 1908, 1912 and 1913, adding the US Open in 1915. Charles "Chick" Evans was another great American amateur player. He won the US Open and the US Amateur in 1916, the first player to win both titles in the same year, and the US Amateur again in 1920.

Charles Blair Macdonald, the first US Amateur Champion, was a formidable figure known for his explosive temper.

Below: Jerry Travers playing out of a bunker. He was US Amateur Champion four times between 1907 and 1913.

"Chick" Evans was one of America's best amateur golfers. He did the double of the US Open and the US Amateur Championship in 1916 and he won the US Amateur Championship again in 1920.

The US Walker Cup team which won by one point at St Andrews in 1926.

Below left: Sam Snead playing at the Open at Carnoustie in 1937.

Below middle: Johnny McDermott, the first native-born American to win the US Open in 1911.

Below right: Laurie Auchterlonie, US Open Champion, 1902.

Francis Ouimet, another amateur, achieved instant fame when he beat Vardon and Ted Ray in 1913 in a play-off at Brookline to win the US Open by five shots. It was billed throughout the USA as a great David and Goliath contest. Ouimet was an unknown twenty-year-old amateur who worked as a caddie at Brookline Country Club. Vardon and Ray were in the USA playing exhibition matches and had just finished first and second in the Open championship in 1912. The US Open was postponed to allow the two to compete and Vardon, who had won the US title in 1900, was acknowledged at that time as the finest player in the world. Ouimet won the US Amateur Championship in 1914 and again 17 years later in 1931.

In the 1920s the amateur and professional game on both sides of the Atlantic was dominated by Bobby Jones. Jones won the US Amateur title five times in seven years from 1924 to 1930 in addition to his three Open and four US Open titles. Another successful American amateur was Lawson Little who won both the British and American titles in 1934 and 1935. He then turned professional and won the US Open in 1940. He started a trend of successful American amateurs turning professional which, in the 1950s and 1960s, saw Palmer and Nicklaus graduate from the amateur ranks.

The American professional golf tournaments started out as adjuncts to the Amateur championships, which were much more popular and attracted bigger entries. At that time golf was played more by the affluent middle and upper classes. The prestige of professionals improved only slowly until the arrival of Hagen, Sarazen and Snead who became national heroes in the 1930s. The first "home-bred" American to win the US Open was Johnny McDermott who won at Chicago in 1911 and repeated his success the following year. Before he made that breakthrough the tournament had been dominated by expatriate Scots like Laurie Auchterlonie, Willie Anderson and the Smith brothers, Alex and Willie. To this day, Willie Anderson is the only person to have won that championship three years in succession. The USA had been waiting for McDermott's win with nationalistic fervour, but it was as nothing compared with Ouimet's success which overnight transformed the popularity of the game. In 1913 fewer than 350,000 people played golf in the USA; ten years later the number had grown to over two million.

In the 1920s and 1930s Americans came to dominate the golfing world on both sides of the Atlantic. The first American winner of the Open was Jock Hutchison in 1921 and he was followed in swift succession by Walter Hagen, "Long" Jim Barnes and Bobby Jones. Indeed Arthur Havers' victory in the Open at Troon in 1923 was the only British success in 13 years before Henry Cotton's first Open victory at Royal St George's in 1934. Bobby Jones won the title three times and Walter Hagen four times. The British Amateur Championship was also won by a number of American golfers: in 1926, Jess Sweetser; 1930, Bobby Jones; 1934 and 1935, Lawson Little; 1937, Robert Sweeny; and 1938, Charlie Yates. The American domination of the game, which was to last until the 1980s, had started.

W. Lawson Little, US and British Amateur Champion in 1934 and 1935 and US Open Champion in 1940. He had a successful career as both an amateur and a professional.

Below: Walter Hagen on the 18th tee at Royal St George's, 1922, when he was about to win the Open Championship.

THE POST-WAR YEARS

The American domination of golf was to continue into the 1940s. The game in Britain slumped in popularity with the administration and prize money falling far behind that in the USA. Ben Hogan came and won the Open in 1953 as Sam Snead had done in 1946, but after that few Americans bothered to come and play in the oldest championship of all. The Open was dominated by Bobby Locke and Peter Thomson, who won it eight times between them between 1949 and 1958, with Thomson adding a fifth title to his tally in 1965.

Locke was a dominant player just after the war and won a number of tournaments in the USA but he was banned from the US Tour in 1949 when he decided to stay in Britain after winning the Open. The USPGA claimed he had violated a number of contracts but there was probably more than a touch of jealousy over his success. Hogan was the leading player in the USA but his success came after that of Byron Nelson who was an exact contemporary of his. Nelson was a great player who won the Masters in 1937 and 1942, the US Open in 1939 and the USPGA Championship in 1940

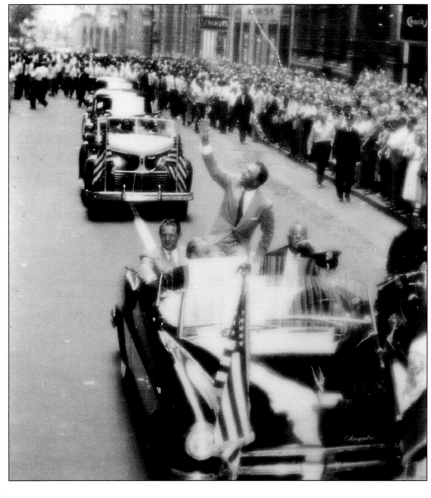

Above: A ticker-tape welcome for Ben Hogan in New York after his triumph in the Open, 1953.

Far left: Byron Nelson, whose best years coincided with the 2nd World War.

Left: Ben Hogan holding the famous claret jug after winning the Open at Carnoustie in 1953.

and 1945. As a haemophiliac, he was not allowed to serve in the armed forces in the war and he continued to play golf to help boost morale in the country. He won 13 out of 23 events on the Tour as it existed in 1944 and in 1945 he won 18 out of the 31 events he entered, coming second in another seven. In that year he had a stroke average of 68.3 per round. He had a friendly rivalry with Ben Hogan which was temporarily settled when he won the Seattle Open in 1945 with a world record score of 259, with Hogan some twenty shots behind. Shortly after that he retired with a chronic stomach illness, though he won the French Open in 1955 on a vacation trip to Europe. He might well have qualified as one of the greatest players the world has ever seen had his career not coincided with the war. Another great American player of the immediate post-war period was Jimmy Demaret who was also a great showman. He won the Masters in 1940, 1947 and 1950. Other names that are frequently remembered are Lloyd Mangrum, winner of the first post-war US Open in 1946 and Cary Middlecoff, who won the US Open in 1949 and the Masters in 1955. These two must hold some sort of

Jimmy Demaret, three times Masters winner, one of the great showmen of American golf.

record: after a tie at the 1949 Detroit Open they played 11 extra holes in a sudden-death play-off in gathering darkness, before giving up and agreeing to share the title.

Below left: Lloyd Mangrum playing out of a bunker, 1950.

Below right: Cary Middlecoff.

THE PALMER YEARS

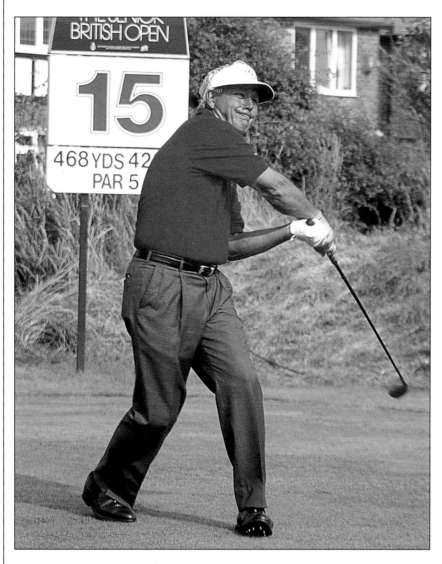

Above: Advancing years have not diminished the ferocity with which Arnold Palmer hits a golf ball.

The centenary Open Championship took place at St Andrews in 1960 and Arnold Palmer came over aiming to win it as a third leg of a golfing Grand Slam; he had already won the Masters and US Open that year. It is a great pity that he did not win: rain postponed the last round and his momentum faded as he finished one stroke behind Kel Nagle. But he vowed to return and to everyone's delight he won the next two Opens at Royal Birkdale in 1961 and Troon in 1962. His presence brought in his wake the leading American players and after 1960 the Open Championship resumed its place as the leading golf competition in the world. Thirty-five years later, Palmer waved farewell to the Open at St Andrews with the applause and affection of the British crowd echoing in his ears. He captured the public imagination on both sides of the Atlantic as no golfer has done before or since. He was exceptionally strong, with huge hands, and his technique was somewhat short of being classic. But what he lacked in finesse he made up for in whole-hearted endeavour. Often, when at the height of his game, he would snatch victory from the jaws of defeat, but as he grew older this happened less frequently. Always, win or lose, he remained polite, charming and enthusiastic.

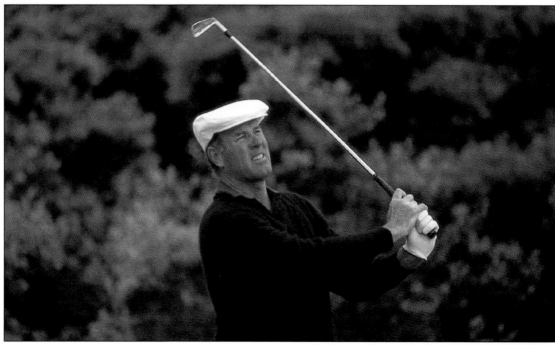

Right: Tom Weiskopf, a beautiful golfer, won the Open at Troon in 1973.

Palmer's advocacy of the Open made golf into an international game. He declared, like Hagen had before him, that the true golfer could play on all types of course and that to be a true champion a golfer had to win the Open on the links courses of Britain, where the game had originated. Hagen had written in his autobiography that he had to change his game completely to win in Britain, adding "I've repeatedly insisted that I like competition. Well, I had it from the links in the British Isles. And far from upsetting me, it challenged my skill as a champion golfer so greatly that I was more and more determined to win that Open Cup".

Where Palmer led his contemporaries followed. Nicklaus, Trevino, Watson, Miller, Weiskopf and Floyd all went on to win in Britain and, as the American challenge grew, so deep down did the spirit of resistance start, first from Jacklin, later from Ballesteros and Faldo. In the last ten years, as golf has become truly international, so the supremacy of the USA has started to show signs of cracking. No-one would say it has been broken but as the twenty-first century approaches golf on both sides of the Atlantic, indeed, throughout the world, is certainly very evenly matched.

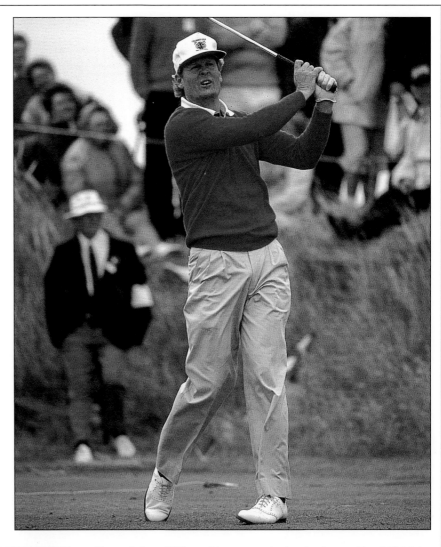

Above: Johnny Miller on his way to winning the Open at Royal Birkdale in 1976. He also won the US Open at Oakmont in 1973.

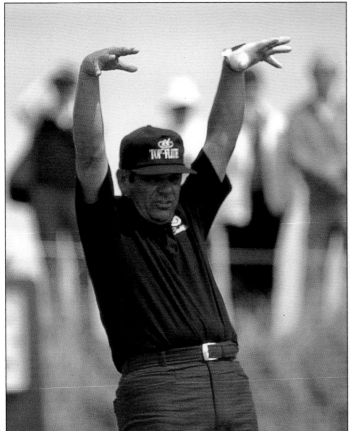

Left: Lee Trevino holing from off the green at the 71st hole of the Open at Muirfield, 1972.

Below: Tony Jacklin, Open Champion in 1969 and first British winner of the US Open since 1920.

WOMEN IN GOLF

Today it might be true to say that as many women play golf as men, and even if it is not, golf is a popular and accepted sport for women. This has not always been the case. Mary, Queen of Scots, was condemned for "playing golf in the fields by Seton" only a few days after the murder of her husband, Darnley. There are pictures of Japanese courtesans playing a game similar to golf several centuries ago. It was not until 1860 that a group of women led by Mrs Robert Boothby, wife of a scratch golfer and member of the Royal and Ancient Club, was discovered playing golf on a caddies' course near St Andrews.

As might have been expected, given the period, a tidal wave of masculine condemnation engulfed the lady golfers. It was not just that ladies were not expected to take any exercise at all but that the posture required to swing a golf club while dressed in long skirts was deemed to be indecorous and unseemly. The links was not a place for women – even as spectators they talked, their dresses rustled in the wind, they did not stand still. However, ladies' golf persisted. The first ladies' golf club was formed at Westward Ho!, Devon, England, in 1868 and around the same time the ladies of St Andrews found a piece of land which was made into a putting course. Dalliance on the tennis court and the croquet lawn was all very well but it paled into insignificance compared with the freedom and opportunities offered by a three-hour golf match on the links. It also helped enormously that the game could be played competitively between the sexes and also between players of vastly different abilities.

The first British Ladies' Championship was played at Lytham St Annes over nine holes in 1893. The winner was Lady Margaret Scott, daughter of Lord Eldon, who had had the advantage of learning how to play on her father's private course. From then on, golf became not only socially acceptable but a sought-after accomplishment. The Ranelagh Club in London promoted golf as a social event under the auspices of the Ladies' Golf Union, which had been formed in 1893 by

Above: The Putting Green, Westward Ho!, from the painting by Sir Francis Grant, 1872.

32.—LADY MARGARET SCOTT. Lady Champion 1893-4-5.

Above and left: Lady Margaret Scott, British Ladies Amateur Champion, 1893-5.

Miss Issette Pearson, a member of the Royal Wimbledon Club. Two years later, in 1895, the first Women's Championship took place in the USA. It was a stroke-play event and was won by Mrs Charles S. Brown.

In the early years of women's golf the leading player in Britain was Lady Margaret Scott, who won the British Ladies' Championship for the first three years and then retired from competitive events. In the USA, it was Beatrix Hoyt, who won the US Women's Championship for three consecutive years from 1896 to 1898 and then also retired. Two other women who had a great influence on golf in the USA and whose surname still features in the world golfing calendar were the sisters Margaret and Harriot Curtis. Harriot Curtis won the US Women's Amateur Championship (the US Women's Open for professionals did not start until 1946) in 1906 and Margaret won it three times in 1907 (when she beat her sister 7 & 6 in the final), 1911 and 1912. They arrived in Britain for the British Women's Championship in 1905, when the first unofficial match between the ladies of Great Britain and the ladies of the USA took place. Another unofficial match took place 25 years later in 1930 and this caused such widespread interest that the Curtis sisters donated a trophy to be played for every two years. The first match was held at Wentworth, England in 1932, and so began the Curtis Cup.

There were two great women golfers on either side of the Atlantic in the early years of the twentieth century, Cecilia (Cecil) Leitch and Alexa Stirling. Cecil Leitch won the British Ladies' title first in 1914 and, after a gap for World War I, again in 1920 and 1921. She added a fourth title in 1926. She had made her name by playing a 72-hole challenge match in 1910 against Harold Hilton, the Open and US Open Champion, at Walton Heath and Sunningdale. Playing off level tees but receiving nine shots a round, she had won by 2 & 1. In the USA, Alexa Stirling, a lifelong friend of Bobby Jones, won the US Women's Amateur Championship three times running in 1916, 1919 and 1920, and she was also runner-up in 1921, 1923 and 1925. However, they were both eclipsed by Joyce Wethered who has many supporters for the title "the greatest golfer that ever lived".

Joyce Wethered was born in 1901 and played her first competition when she was eighteen, reaching the last four in the Surrey Ladies' Championship. The following year she entered the English Ladies' Championship and beat Cecil Leitch in the final by 2 & 1.

Above and left: Cecil Leitch, the great rival of Joyce Wethered, won the British Ladies' Amateur Championship four times between 1914 and 1926.

She had been six down with 16 holes to play. This was the match, played at Sheringham, when she was asked whether she had not been put off by the train which rattled past as she was preparing to take an important putt; "What train?" was her reply. This win in the English Ladies' was the first of five consecutive successes. After her win in 1924 she never competed in that event again. Her record in the British Ladies' Championship is incomparable. Beaten by Cecil Leitch in the final of 1921 she took her revenge in 1922 by the record margin of 9 & 7 and then won again in 1924 and 1925. After that victory she retired. Shy and nervous, the strain of playing at the top level was too much. She was just twenty-four.

Above and left: Joyce Wethered, long after she had retired from competitive golf.

In the years between 1925 and 1929 the centre of ladies' golfing excellence passed to the USA where Glenna Collett became the undisputed champion. She had won the US Women's title four times since 1922 and in 1929, after a second successive victory, made a bid for the British Ladies' Championship which had never been won by a foreigner before. The championship was to be played at St Andrews and Joyce Wethered was persuaded to come out of retirement to compete. Rarely in life are expectations fulfilled so precisely. Drawn in opposite halves of the field, the champion of America and the former champion of Britain won their way into the final, which attracted a crowd of more than five thousand people. After nine holes Collett, playing superb golf, was five holes up. Joyce Wethered refused to give in and won by 3 & 1 on the penultimate green. Her return to the clubhouse accompanied by policemen through wildly cheering crowds left her emotionally drained and exhausted. Feeling she had nothing left to prove, she retired again. There was, however, one final comeback. In 1932 she played in the first Curtis Cup match and beat Glenna Collett 6 & 4 in the top singles.

In 1934 Wethered went to work in the golfing department of Fortnum & Mason in London and as a result the Ladies' Golf Union revoked her amateur status. After this, she went to the USA and played a series of exhibition matches around the country against Bobby Jones, Gene Sarazen, Walter Hagen and her old rival, Glenna Collett. Later she returned to England and in 1937 she married Sir John Heathcoat-Amory. Her amateur status was restored in 1947.

The other legendary woman player was born Mildred Didrikson, but is much better known as "Babe" Zaharias. She was one of the greatest athletes, man or woman, there has ever been. She started as a baseball and basketball player and obtained her nickname because she once hit five home runs in one game, thus inviting comparison with the great Babe Ruth. When she was eighteen she entered the National Track and Field Championships before the Olympic Games and won six events, setting new world records in four of them. In the 1932 Olympic Games in Los Angeles she won gold medals in the

Glenna Collett, six times US Women's Amateur Champion between 1922 and 1935, another great rival of Joyce Wethered.

javelin, the high hurdles and the high jump, but she was disqualified from the high jump after setting a new world record because she has used the "Western Roll", a new technique which was then considered to be unladylike. During the Los Angeles games she was persuaded to try golf, a game at which she was instantly successful. She won the second tournament that she entered but then she was disqualified by the USGA as they held that her

"Babe" Zaharias holding the British Ladies' Amateur trophy after her win at Gullane in 1947.

earnings as a basketball and baseball player meant she was a professional player. As with Joyce Wethered before her, the amateur game, which at that time was the only game available, was barred to her. "Babe" Didrikson married George Zaharias in 1938 and regained her amateur status five years later. She then proceeded to win 17 consecutive tournaments, including the British Ladies' Amateur in 1947. She was the first American winner of this event. Later that year she turned professional and was a leading figure in establishing the LPGA. She won 31 events on the tour, including five after a cancer operation in 1953, and two more, including the last of her three US Women's Opens, in 1954. Sadly, the cancer recurred and she died the following year.

There have been other great champions: Mickey Wright, winner of 82 events on the US LPGA tour, including a record four US Women's Opens and four LPGA Championships; Kathy Whitworth, the most prolific winner of all time on the US circuit, but who never won the US Women's Open; Patty Berg, Pat Bradley, Amy Alcott, JoAnne Carner and Nancy Lopez. Today, Laura Davies of Britain, leader of the Ping World Rankings, and the young Swede, Annika Sorenstam, are the leading names in women's golf and set the standards to which others aspire. The four major tournaments for women are the US Women's Open, the McDonalds LPGA Championship, the du Maurier Classic and the Nabisco Dinah Shore.

The women's game has come a long way since 1860 when Mrs Robert Boothby first played in public on the caddies' course at St Andrews. There are established women's tours on both sides of the Atlantic, though the American tour is much the largest both in monetary terms and the number of events played. In 1995 Annika Sorenstam and Laura Davies led the money list on both tours and women's golf continues to increase in popularity and sponsorship. More television coverage, particularly in Europe, will no doubt assist this in the future.

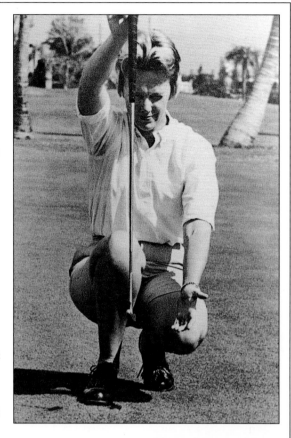

Mickey Wright, one of the most prolific winners on the US women's tour with 82 victories including eight majors.

Far left: Annika Sorenstam, leading money winner on the women's tour in Europe and America in 1995.

Left: Laura Davies, the hugely popular British player, who is one of the most successful women golfers of the 1990s.

CHAPTER 2

FAMOUS GOLFERS

The history of golf is illuminated by its players and their skills. This is a brief celebration of just some of those founding fathers who helped the sport achieve its status, and of the personalities of the present that make the game a joy to follow.

Greg Norman holds the renowned claret jug after his Open win in 1993.

Bobby Jones drives through a New York ticker-tape welcome after winning the Open Championship in 1926.

ALLAN ROBERTSON

Allan Robertson, the first man to break 80 at the Old Course, St Andrews, is reputed never to have lost a golf match.

Allan Robertson (1815–1859) was the first golfer to gain public recognition. He was the first man to break 80 on the Old Course at St Andrews, which he did in 1858. At that time such a score was considered a marvel. Robertson came from a family of professional golfers who made "featheries" at St Andrews. Indeed, when the gutta-percha ball arrived Robertson would have nothing to do with it and this caused a rift with "Old" Tom Morris who was apprenticed to him at the time. Robertson is reputed never to have lost a match. Whether this is strictly true is doubtful but it is certain that he lost very few and he was never beaten when partnered by "Old" Tom Morris. Their most famous match was against the Dunn brothers when, after being four down with eight to play, they won the final two holes of a three-cornered contest at North Berwick to win by two holes.

Robertson died after contracting jaundice in 1859, the year before the first Open Championship. When his death was announced, a member of the Royal and Ancient Club declared, "They may shut up their shops and toll their bells, for the greatest among them is gone".

"OLD" TOM MORRIS

"Old" Tom Morris, four times Open Champion, 1861-1867. His bust is on the R & A clubhouse at St Andrews.

"Old" Tom Morris (1821–1908), so-called to distinguish him from his son "Young" Tom, was apprenticed to Allan Robertson at St Andrews as a ballmaker and soon started to partner him on the golf course. He quarrelled with Robertson, however, over the introduction of the gutta-percha ball and left St Andrews to become greenkeeper at Prestwick in 1851. He was instrumental in arranging the first Open Championship which was played at Prestwick in 1860. Although favourite to win, he finished runner-up to Willie Park Snr, losing by two strokes. "Old" Tom Morris gained his revenge the following year when he completed the three rounds on the 12-hole course in 163 strokes and he won again in 1862, 1864 and 1867. In 1868, he gave way to his son "Young" Tom, who was the most brilliant player of his or possibly any other generation. "Old" Tom is reputed to have said, "I could cope wi' Allan (Robertson) myself, but never wi' Tommy". "Old" Tom

returned to St Andrews in 1865 as greenkeeper and then professional to the Royal and Ancient Golf Club, a post he held until his death. He died in 1908, aged 87, after falling down the staircase at the new clubhouse. A kindly and much-loved man, no golf was played at St Andrews on the day of his funeral in honour of his memory. His bust looks down on the first tee from the front of the Royal and Ancient clubhouse to this day.

"YOUNG" TOM MORRIS

"Young" Tom (1851–1875) first won the Open in 1868 at the age of seventeen, and remains the youngest player ever to win it. In that tournament he also recorded the first hole-in-one in the competition. He won again in 1869 and 1870, when his winning score for the 36 holes was 149, including an eagle 3 at the first hole in the final round. This was incredible scoring and his total was not equalled for the next 32 years when the guttie ball was in use. Having retained the champion's belt outright for his three consecutive wins, the championship lapsed in 1871 as the Prestwick Club rather embarrassingly had no trophy to play for. But when it was resumed in 1872, "Young" Tom recorded his fourth successive victory. He thus became the first winner of the famous claret jug, which is still held up by every winner and has the most famous names in the history of golf inscribed on its plinth. He was runner-up to Mungo Park in 1874 when the tournament was played at Musselburgh. Tragically, "Young" Tom died of a broken heart the following year after his wife had died in childbirth; he was twenty-four. There is a memorial to him in the grounds of St Rule's Cathedral, St Andrews.

26.—TOM MORRIS, JNR.

"Young" Tom Morris, the youngest-ever winner of the Open Championship in 1868 when he was seventeen.

WILLIE PARK JUNIOR

Willie Park Junior (1864–1925) won the Open Championship twice, in 1887 and 1889, and was the son of Willie Park who won the inaugural Open Championship in 1860 and then succeeded again in 1863, 1866 and 1875. His uncle, Mungo Park, beat "Young" Tom Morris in 1874. Willie Park Junior played many challenge matches, which were very popular at that time, and designed a number of golf courses. He also invented a 56-sided golf ball and wrote the first complete book on golf by a professional, *The Game of Golf*, published 1896.

Willie Park Junior, member of a great golfing family.

A man playing in the medal round came to the last green to find his ball lying beyond the hole, presenting him with a long and tricky downhill putt. At that moment a friend came out of the clubhouse and said, "If you hole that you'll tie for second place." After a long careful study of the putt from both sides of the hole the golfer marched up to his ball, picked it up and walked into the clubhouse saying, "I can't hole it."

THE GREAT TRIUMVIRATE

Right: Harry Vardon lining up a putt.

John Taylor, Harry Vardon and James Braid were known as the "Great Triumvirate" and in the 21 years from 1894 to the start of World War I they won the Open Championship no fewer than 16 times between them.

JOHN TAYLOR

Taylor, always known as "J. H.", first played in the Open in 1893 when he was twenty-two. He won it the following year when it was played at Royal St George's, which was the first time the championship had been played in England and, appropriately enough, he was the first English winner. In total, he won the Open five times. He was also runner-up on three occasions, won the French Open in 1908 and 1909, the German Open in 1912, and was runner-up to Harry Vardon in the US Open of 1900. "J. H." was instrumental in setting up the British Professional Golfers' Association and was a much-honoured figure in the world of golf. He was made an honorary member of the Royal and Ancient Golf Club, which presented him with a commemorative silver salver on his ninetieth birthday in 1961.

HARRY VARDON

Harry Vardon, the second member of the triumvirate, is known as the inventor of the Vardon overlapping grip, which he popularized but probably did not invent. He won the Open a record six times with his first victory coming in 1896 and his last, when he was forty-four, in 1914. He played countless exhibition matches and also won the US Open in 1900, when he spent a year touring the United States promoting his new ball, the "Vardon Flyer". In fact, the ball, one of the last generation of gutta-percha balls, was soon superseded by the Haskell rubber-cored ball. Vardon became very ill in 1903 with tuberculosis and never really played at his best again. However, such terms are relative, as he won the Open in 1911 and 1914, and finished joint runner-up in the US Open in 1920 when he was fifty. At the height of his game he was said to be two strokes a round better than Taylor and Braid, and he was such a fine striker of a golf ball that he is reputed in an afternoon round to have driven into the divot marks he had made in the morning. He is said to have suffered from the "yips", the jerk which afflicts many players when confronted with a three-foot putt, in his final years.

JAMES BRAID

James Braid is the last and perhaps the least-known of the famous three. Nevertheless, he was the first man to win the Open five times, which he did between the years 1901 and 1910. Surprisingly for a Scot, he established his reputation in England. He started his career as a clubmaker at the Army and Navy Stores in London in 1893, and was for many years associated with the Walton Heath Golf Club in Surrey. As well as his Open victories he also won the first match-play professional tournament in 1903, a victory he repeated another three times in the next eight years. He was a modest and unassuming man, a founder member of the PGA and an accomplished golf course architect. He designed the King's Course at Gleneagles.

WALTER HAGEN

In the aftermath of World War I, the centre of golfing excellence passed from England and Scotland across the water to the USA. The American approach to golf was embodied by Walter Hagen (1892-1969) who turned the whole world of professional golf upside-down. He was an instinctive showman. The best story about him was of when he arrived at Deal to play in the 1920 Open Championship. Professional golfers were not allowed in the clubhouse, so Hagen hired a Daimler, together with a chauffeur and footman, parked it outside the clubhouse front door and had the footman collect his belongings each day when he arrived at the 18th hole. Two years later, in 1922, he won the Open Championship for the first time and he won again in 1924, 1928 and 1929, was runner-up to Arthur Havers at Troon in 1923 and

third behind Bobby Jones and Al Watrous at Lytham in 1926. He won the US Open in 1914 and 1919, and the USPGA five times, including four successive years from 1924. Hagen's record was truly remarkable. He was the first international golfer to play in comfortable, stylish clothing, usually bright sweaters and plusfours. Stories about him are legendary and his prowess is best summed up by the remark of Bernard Darwin, the great golf writer, "The difference between Hagen and other players is that he just wins and they don't"

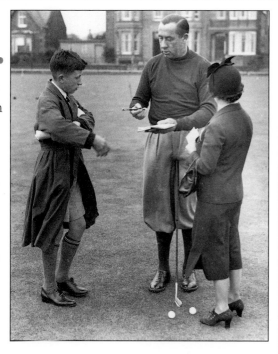

Walter Hagen signing autographs at St Andrews, in 1933.

BOBBY JONES

While there may be dispute as to whether Bobby Jones (1902–1971) was the greatest golfer there has ever been, there are few who would argue that he is the greatest amateur player the world has ever seen. Jones, however, did not consider himself to be the best for when asked, at the height of his fame, "What does it feel like to be the greatest player in the world?" he modestly replied, "I don't know – the best player in the world is a woman," referring to Joyce Wethered. But his record speaks for itself: in seven years from 1923, Jones won the US Open four times, the Open three times, the US Amateur Championship five times and the British Amateur Championship in 1930, the year in which he completed a Grand Slam by winning all four.

After he had won the US Amateur at Merion, Jones retired from competitive golf at the age of twenty-eight. He founded the Augusta National Golf Club, the permanent home of the US Masters, and in 1958 he was

made a freeman of St Andrews, the highest honour that could be bestowed on him. In 1936, six years after he had last played golf competitively, he played a round at St Andrews as an ordinary player where he had won the 1927 Open. When word got around that Bobby Jones was playing, the townsfolk turned out in force. The crowd at the first tee was over 2,000 and the numbers swelled as his round progressed. Later, confined to a wheelchair, he wrote of his welcome that day, adding, "I could take out of my life everything except my experiences at St Andrews and I'd still have had a full and rich life"

There is a famous story which illustrates the carefree nature of Walter Hagen. He loved a party. Playing in the Open at Muirfield in 1929, which he won, he went to a card game which lasted into the early hours of the morning. At 3 or 4 a.m. one of his supporters, thinking it time that Hagen got some sleep, said that Leo Diegel, Hagen's nearest rival, had been in bed for several hours. "He won't be asleep," Hagen replied.

Bobby Jones, from a portrait painted in 1930, the year of the Grand Slam.

GENE SARAZEN

CHURCHMAN'S CIGARETTES

E. SARAZEN

Gene Sarazen, the first player to win the four majors.

Gene Sarazen was born in 1902 and started out as an assistant professional at the Fort Wayne club because he had been advised to work out of doors. He entered the US Open in 1920 and his entry fee was paid by the members. Two years later he won the title and also the USPGA Championship, which was then still a match-play event. He was only twenty. Sarazen won the USPGA again the following year but after that he experienced a period in the wilderness when

he experimented with his swing, trying to compensate for his height which was only 5 ft 4 in (1.63 m). In 1930 he was runner-up in the USPGA and then crossed the Atlantic to win the Open in 1932. The Masters tournament had started in 1934 and Sarazen entered for the first time the following year. Craig Wood was the leader in the clubhouse with a total of 282 when Sarazen stood on the 15th tee in his final round. He required two birdies in the last four holes to tie with Wood, three to win. On the 15th hole, after a good drive, he hit a 4-wood 235 yards (215m) across the water guarding the green, which rolled across the green and into the hole. He had an albatross 2 and after three pars to tie with Wood he won the play-off the next day by five shots. This made Sarazen the first player to win the four major tournaments: the Open, the US Open, the USPGA Championship and the Masters. Most people will remember him when he returned to Troon in 1973 to play in the Open, 50 years after the year when, as US Open champion, he had failed to qualify there. In full view of everybody and recorded for posterity on the television, he holed in one at the famous "Postage Stamp", 8th hole.

HENRY COTTON

Sir Henry Cotton, knighted in 1987 for his services to golf, started the golf school at Penina.

Henry Cotton (1907-1987) was the best British golfer of his day, and since the days of Braid and Vardon few have matched his achievements. He won the Open at Royal St George's in 1934 where his first round of 65 set a course record. The well-known golf ball Dunlop 65 is named in commemoration of this achievement. His win came after 12 years of American domination of this great event. Cotton won the Open again in 1937 and 1948. If all sporting events had not been cancelled during World War II, Cotton may well have been the first four-times British winner of the Open since Harry Vardon won his last championship in 1914.

SAM SNEAD

Sam Snead won every important tournament in the world except the US Open, where he finished runner-up four times. His luck in this tournament was cruel. In 1939, needing a 5 to win at the last hole, he took an 8, and in 1947 he lost a play-off to Lew Worsham by one shot. He continued winning tournaments until he was in his sixties and finished third in the USPGA in 1974 when he was 62, behind Lee Trevino and Jack Nicklaus. Sam Snead was largely self-taught and the secret of his continuing success was his beautiful swing, which never let him down. His first major success came when he won the USPGA in 1942. He won the first Open after the war in 1946, the Masters three times, the USPGA twice more, in 1949 and

"Slamming" Sam Snead with the Open trophy in 1946.

1951, and founded the USPGA Seniors Tour where he won the title six times between 1964 and 1973. Later in life he suffered from the "yips" and developed his "sidewinder" putting technique as a result.

One golfer's triumph is so often another's disaster and Kipling's "twin imposters" have to be treated the same. Sam Snead came to the 72nd hole of the US Open in 1939 needing a 5 to win. He took 8. Jack Maclean, the British Walker Cup player, came to the final hole of the 1936 US Amateur Championship one-up. Johnny Fischer, his opponent, holed in 2 to square the match and then birdied the first extra hole to win. Fischer's triumph, Maclean's disaster.

BEN HOGAN

Ben Hogan was a slow starter. He turned professional in 1931 but it took seven years for him to win his first tournament. But in the years after the War he was indisputably the finest golfer in the world and at his peak one of the best there has ever been. Hogan won his first major title, the USPGA, in 1946. He won it again in 1948 and in that year he also won the US Open. In February 1949 he had a horrific car accident and was so badly injured that he was at first told he would never walk again, let alone play golf. Hogan thought differently: slowly he rebuilt his shattered body and then in 1950 he started to play golf again. His comeback was remarkable; he won the US Open that year and the following year both the US Open and the Masters, a double he repeated in 1953. In 1953 he decided to play in the Open, even though he was a most reluctant traveller, and it was the only time he played in that event. The Championship was held that year at Carnoustie, which is arguably the toughest of all British championship courses. Neither Hogan nor the crowds of American journalists who followed their hero had ever seen anything like it. Hogan opened with a 73 and then progressively shot 71, 70 and 68 for victory. No man, before or since, has ever won three of the major titles in the same year. If the USPGA had not still been a match-play event played over 36 holes a day he would probably have won that as well, but he did not enter as he thought it would be too much of a strain on his injured legs. Although Hogan continued playing, he never again touched such heights and his putting started to give him trouble. He remains, however, one of the greatest players of all time and perhaps the finest striker of a golf ball there has ever been.

Ben Hogan, one of the greatest golfers of all.

BOBBY LOCKE

Bobby Locke, four times Open Champion.

Sir Horace Rumbold, the distinguished diplomat, was playing golf against his nephew, who was a fine player with a handicap of two. The nephew had been given strict instructions that the match was not to be too one-sided and by the time they reached the 17th hole a combination of deliberately sliced drives and topped iron shots ensured that he was only one-up. Sir Horace then said, "You know, Bobby, all my life people have looked at me and thought that I was stupid. But I'll tell you one thing, I'm not as stupid as I look."

Peter Thomson, winner of the Open three years in succession from 1954-6.

Bobby Locke (1917-1987) is considered to be one of the best players ever to come from South Africa. He started playing as an amateur at a very early age and won the South African Open five times in six years from 1935 to 1940. After the war, in which he served as a bomber pilot in the South African Air Force, he went to the United States and played in 59 tournaments in just over two years, winning no fewer than 13 of them and finishing runner-up in a further ten. This was a magnificent achievement by any standards. Locke then returned to Europe where he won the Open four times in 1949, 1950, 1952 and 1957. He was a flamboyant figure on the golf course, usually dressed in large plus-fours and a white cap, but was not popular. At one stage he was barred from the US tour and was memorably accused of slow play. Locke's reply to this was to wager that he was the fastest player in the world, provided that he was timed from when he arrived six feet away from his ball to after he had played his shot. He had a car accident in 1959 which damaged his eyesight and he played little competitive golf after that date.

PETER THOMSON

There is a question mark against Peter Thomson as one of the world's great golfers. Perhaps this is because his triumphs came in a period when few Americans played in Europe and because of his relative lack of success when he played in the US. However, his record as winner of five Open Championships has only been equalled by Tom Watson this century and no-one has won three consecutive Open Championships since "Young" Tom Morris. Thomson's wins came in 1954, 1955, 1956 and 1958, missing out in 1957 when he was beaten into second place by Bobby Locke, and finally in 1965 when he beat the defending champion Tony Lema at Royal Birkdale – his finest victory. Thomson was the most relaxed player, orthodox and controlled, only lacking a certain length from the tee, which handicapped him when he played in the US. However, he played on the USPGA Seniors Tour in the early 80s, winning a number of tournaments.

ARNOLD PALMER

The world of golf owes a great debt to Arnold Palmer. Single-handedly, he fashioned the modern international game and his charisma was such that he has justly become the most popular player the world has ever seen. Few who witnessed it could not be moved by his emotional farewell to the Open Championship at St Andrews where he competed for the last time in 1995. It was Palmer who revived the Open, which had become a purely European championship, in the early 1960s. He won at Royal Birkdale in 1961 and at Troon in 1962, with a masterly exhibition of golf. His example encouraged the other top professionals in the US to compete in the greatest championship of all. As a player, Palmer made the purists shudder; he had a quick, short, rather graceless swing but he was immensely strong, with a swashbuckling, all-or-nothing attitude that captured the imagination of the world: "If I can see it, I can hit it, and if I can hit it, I can hole it." As well as his two Opens, Palmer won the Masters four times, and was second twice, he won the US Open in 1960 and the only major which eluded him was the USPGA Championship. He was for years one of the leading players on the USPGA Seniors Tour. Graceful, charming and always polite, Palmer has been an ideal role model for countless young golfers all over the world.

Arnold Palmer, one of the most charismatic golfers of all.

GARY PLAYER

Gary Player is certainly one of the great players of the modern era, with a record second only to Jack Nicklaus. A man of iron determination, he spent countless hours practising and when asked once about a "lucky" shot he had holed from a bunker replied, "It's a funny thing, the more I practise the luckier I get". The first tournament of note that he won was the Dunlop Masters at Sunningdale in 1955 at the age of twenty and the following year he won the first of 13 South African Open titles. He also won the Australian Open seven times. His record in the majors is also outstanding and not just in the number of victories but the manner in which they were achieved. His first major championship was the Open at Muirfield in 1959 when his last two rounds of 70 and 68 gave him a two-shot victory. He then became the first non-American player to win the Masters in 1961, which he won twice more in 1974 and 1978, when he came from nowhere in the final round with seven birdies in the last ten holes. He also won the USPGA in 1962 and 1972 and the US Open in 1965, and so became one of the greats who have won all four majors. Perhaps his most memorable win was his second Open at Carnoustie in 1968 when he beat Jack Nicklaus and Bob Charles into second place. He won a third Open in 1974. Player was also the supreme exponent of match-play, winning the World Matchplay Championship five times between 1965 and 1973, including one of the greatest golf matches ever played, against Tony Lema. He is a living testimony to the virtues of fitness, practice, determination and hard work.

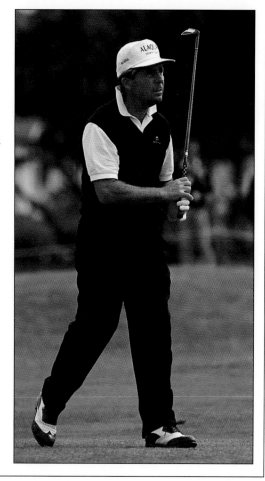

Gary Player is often known as "the man in black" from his habit of wearing black clothes.

LEE TREVINO

Lee Trevino, one of the great characters of golf, had a magical touch around the green.

Lee Trevino is a folk hero. He came from the humblest background and, although he played golf during his service in the marines, he started as a hustler playing with one club, a 3-iron. He is reputed to have said of this time: "Pressure is when you are playing for $10 and you only have $3 in your pocket". He started playing full time on the US Tour in 1967 when he was named "Rookie of the Year". In 1968 he astonished the world by winning the US Open, beating Jack Nicklaus by four shots and breaking 70 in every round, the first time this had been done. He won the Open, Canadian Open and US Open in 1971, all within the space of a memorable 21 days, and the USPGA title in 1974 and 1984. His second Open title came in 1972 at Muirfield when he shattered the British champion Tony Jacklin by chipping in twice from off the green and holing a bunker shot. "God," remarked Trevino, "is Mexican". Trevino was known for his constant good humour and wisecracks, which at times could be distracting to the players he was paired with. One British professional asked not to be paired with him and when Tony Jacklin asked whether their match at Wentworth could be played with a degree of silence, Trevino replied, "Sure, you don't have to say a word – you just have to listen". The only major title that eluded him was the Masters because his game, with a pronounced fade, did not really suit the course at Augusta. Trevino has continued playing on the Seniors Tour with great success and his talents as a communicator are now heard on television.

JACK NICKLAUS

Above: A youthful Jack Nicklaus.

Right: After thirty years at the top, Jack Nicklaus is still competing.

For many the greatest golfer the world has ever seen, Jack Nicklaus epitomizes the best of the game. He is also a great golf-course architect and designer. His course at his home town, named Muirfield Village after the great course on the Firth of Forth, has hosted the Ryder Cup. He was an immensely talented player as a young man and won the US Amateur Championship in 1959 when he was just nineteen. The following year he came second to Arnold Palmer in the US Open. Nicklaus turned professional in 1962 and won the US Open that year, followed by the Masters and USPGA Championship in 1963. He won his first Open in 1966 and then again in 1970 and 1978. In all, Nicklaus has won 18 major titles, the last one being the Masters in 1986 at the age of forty-six. Almost as astonishing as his successes are the number of times he has finished second, and his duel with Tom Watson at Turnberry in 1977 will be remembered as one of the great golf contests of all time. At the outset of his career

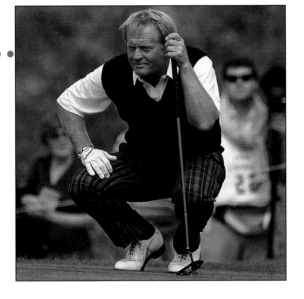

Nicklaus was not a popular figure in the USA because he threatened the reign of the hero, Arnold Palmer. But as the years have passed he has established a strong hold on the affections of the whole golfing world. At his prime, his game was unsurpassed, and was based on intense concentration and great length from the tee. Only Sam Snead has won more tournaments in the USA and Nicklaus has been the leading player on the Seniors Tour now for a number of years.

TONY JACKLIN

There was a time when Tony Jacklin looked as if he would become one of the truly great golfers of all time. That he failed to achieve such heights can probably be attributed to the outrageous fortune or, to put it another way, the outstanding skill, of Lee Trevino, who overtook him in the last two holes of the Open at Muirfield in 1972, when Jacklin looked a certain winner for the second time. Jacklin was never the same again. After an apprenticeship in Europe, Jacklin joined the American tour and won the Jacksonville Open in 1968, which was the first time a British player had won an American event since the war. He followed this by winning the Open at Royal Lytham and St Annes in 1969 and the US Open in 1970, becoming only the third non-American winner and the first British winner since Harry Vardon in 1900.

He held both titles at the same time. The best golf Jacklin ever played was at the start of the Open at St Andrews in 1970 when he went to the turn in 29 strokes and then birdied the 10th. There was then a violent thunderstorm, the greens were flooded and play was halted on the 14th green. When Jacklin returned the next day the magic was gone.

Tony Jacklin (right) and Ray Floyd, captains of the two teams, after the tied Ryder Cup match at The Belfry, 1989.

TOM WATSON

It would probably be true that a record sixth Open win for Tom Watson would be more popular in Britain than any win for a home player, such is the affection and admiration with which he is held in that country. He first won the Open at Carnoustie in 1975, beating Jack Newton in a play-off. He then beat Jack Nicklaus in a memorable duel at Turnberry in 1977. He won again in 1980 and, although he missed out in 1981, he won in consecutive years in 1982 and 1983. All but one of his victories were in Scotland on the great links courses. When he won his fifth Open he equalled the number of victories of J. H. Taylor, James Braid and Peter Thomson. On his own side of the Atlantic, Watson won the Masters in 1977 and 1981, and the US Open in 1982. He has never won the USPGA Championship and so has not achieved the Grand Slam of all four majors won by Nicklaus, Player, Sarazen and Hogan. It is ironic that the fortunes of Watson's career changed at the greatest hole on probably his favourite course. In 1984 at St Andrews, Watson was tied for the lead with Severiano Ballesteros with two holes to play. At the 17th, the "Road" hole, after a perfect drive, adrenalin pumping, his second shot was too strong and finished over the green against the wall. He failed to get up and down in two as so many have before him and when Ballesteros birdied the last hole he won by two shots. All of a sudden, Watson, previously one of the best putters in the world, started having putting problems. His finest days were over.

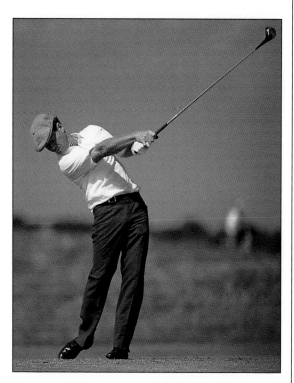

Tom Watson, five times winner of The Open, 1975-1983.

SEVERIANO BALLESTEROS

Severiano Ballesteros, Spain's finest ever golfer.

Any list of great golfers must include Severiano Ballesteros, or "Seve" as he is known the world over, even though his tally of major tournaments is less than at one time it seemed it would be. He burst on the golfing scene aged nineteen at Royal Birkdale when he finished second in the Open, tying with Jack Nicklaus behind Johnny Miller. In 1979 he won the first of his three Opens and won the Masters in 1980 and 1983. At the height of his powers he was an enormously exciting player, hitting the ball vast distances from the tee, not always dead straight, and then manufacturing miraculous recovery shots. In addition to the majors, Seve has won 46 European Tour events and the World Matchplay Championship on four occasions. There is no doubt that he would have won more often but for a back problem which has restricted his swing for a number of years. He is perhaps best known for his advocacy of the Ryder Cup, which, after the inclusion of players from all European countries, has become a competition ferociously contested every two years between the top golfers in the USA and Europe. His record as an inspiration to the team has been outstanding and he is due to be captain of the European team in 1997, when the event will be held at his home course at Valderrama.

NICK FALDO

Nick Faldo is an enigma. For much of his career he has seemed tortured by self-doubt, which has sometimes shown itself as petulance with the press and public, but there can be no denying that he is the most successful player in the world at a time when the competition at the top grows harder each year. He has also had to carry the monumental weight of British expectation that he is a likely winner of every golfing major. Nick Faldo showed his talent early when he won the English Amateur Championship shortly after his eighteenth birthday. He was a consistent winner in Europe and even won tournaments in the USA, but in 1983 he decided that his swing, which had often been admired for its length and smoothness, was not consistent enough to enable him to win under real pressure at the top. When he was in the USA he met David Leadbetter, a British golf coach who was based in Florida. Leadbetter changed his swing and this remodelling took place over a two-year period during which time Faldo dropped to 42nd in the European Order of Merit. However, it paid dividends; Faldo won the Open at Muirfield in 1987 with a much talked-about final round of 18 consecutive pars. He then won back-to-back Masters titles in 1989 and 1990, winning both these titles at the second extra hole in play-offs, the 11th at Augusta, which he described as his favourite hole in all golf. A second Open followed in 1990 at St Andrews and a third at Royal St George's, Sandwich, in 1992. Faldo's finest triumph was at the Masters in 1996. Entering the final round six strokes behind the tournament leader Greg Norman, the World Number One, he made up 11 shots, going round in 67 as Norman unaccountably collapsed to a 78 and defeat by five shots. No-one who witnessed that dramatic turnaround could not have been impressed, not only by the icy composure that he showed on the course but with the genuine respect and affection that he accorded the loser on the 18th green. As he approaches forty, Faldo's best years may lie ahead of him.

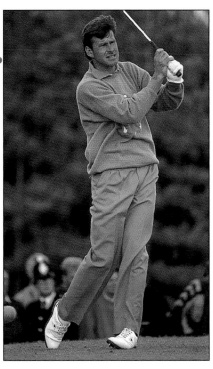

Nick Faldo, whose search for perfection on the golf course has brought him six major titles.

GREG NORMAN

Greg Norman, who has been World Number One longer than any other golfer.

Greg Norman has been the World Number One more often and for longer than any other golfer in an age when the competition from all corners of the world is fiercer than ever. He is one of the longest and straightest hitters there has ever been. He has an excellent short game, honed by hours of practice. He has a charismatic personality and, as "The Great White Shark", always attracts huge galleries to watch him play. However, to date, he has won the Open only twice, first at Turnberry in 1986 when he equalled the tournament record with a 63, and again in 1993 at Royal St George's, and no other major. His record in these has been marked by a series of catastrophes. Bob Tway chipped in from a bunker to beat him in the USPGA Championship in 1986 when he had held a big lead with just nine holes left to play. Larry Mize chipped in at Augusta to beat him in a play-off at the Masters in 1987. He lost a play-off for the Open in 1989, when it was won by Mark Calcavecchia. He lost a play-off for the USPGA in 1993 to Paul Azinger and he was second in the US Open to Corey Pavin in 1995. In the 1996 Masters he led by six shots from Nick Faldo at the start of the final round but blew up and lost by five shots. All things are relative, yet it is difficult to avoid the conclusion that when it really comes to the crunch Norman has flaws, either of technique or temperament, which prevent him succeeding at the highest level of the game.

BERNHARD LANGER

Bernhard Langer, twice winner of the Masters, the best golfer Germany has produced.

Bernhard Langer is the best golfer ever to come from Germany. Indeed, he was the first German to win the German Open Championship, which he did in 1981. He has won the Masters twice, in 1985 and 1993, been second twice in the Open and won countless other tournaments all over the world. His career has been dogged by the "yips", the dreaded jerk which afflicts many players confronted with a three-foot putt, and in his career he has found three different cures, the last of which involves him gripping the putter left hand below right, with the right hand clamping the putter handle to his left forearm. His determination to overcome this trouble is typical of a tenacity that makes him such a dangerous adversary on the course. It was unfortunate for him that he was the player who missed the four-foot putt that meant the Ryder Cup returned to the USA in 1991 at Kiawah Island.

FUTURE CHAMPIONS

Any list of the greatest players is invidious and many fine players, past and present, have been excluded from this chapter because of space. Who will be the next golfing superstar? John Daly has already won two majors and hits the ball so far that on his day he makes every golf-course architect there has ever been look ridiculous. Phil Mickleson may well turn out to be the greatest left-hander of all time, while Colin Montgomerie of Scotland is already the most consistent player day-in, day-out in Europe but has sometimes shown "Norman-like" tendencies to let the really big occasion get away from him.

CHAPTER 3

THE GREAT TOURNAMENTS

It is through watching the great play their tournaments that the less talented golfers among us are inspired to keep trying to improve our game. Their talent, skill and tenacity when playing against each other are endlessly watchable, live at the course or on television.

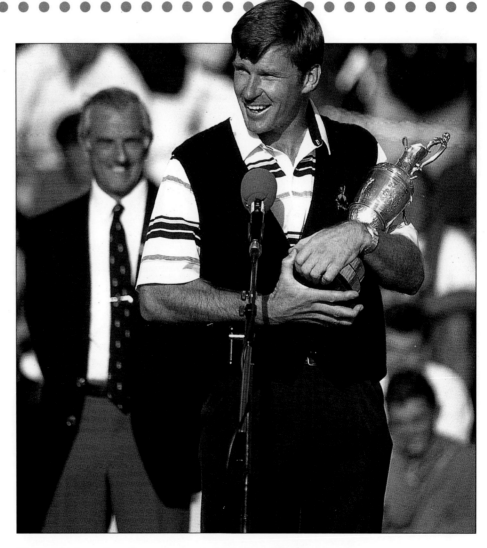

Nick Faldo, three-times Open winner, after his win at St Andrews in 1990.

Augusta, the first great major event of the golfing year

THE GREAT TOURNAMENTS

"Old" and "Young" Tom Morris; between them they won the Open eight times.

Below: Vast crowds cluster round the final green at Royal Birkdale, 1991.

There are four major tournaments each year; the Open, usually just called the Open, the US Open, the Masters and the USPGA. To win one of these titles is to achieve one of the summits in golf. Only four players, Nicklaus, Player, Hogan and Sarazen, have won all four. However, this is a slightly misleading statistic as the Masters was first played in 1934. Vardon, Barnes, Walter Hagen, Bobby Jones and both Morrises won every tournament of their day. Of those who won three out of four, Arnold Palmer never won the USPGA, Lee Trevino never won the Masters, Tom Watson has never won the USPGA, Sam Snead never won the US Open, Byron Nelson never won the Open, though he might have done if World War II had not intervened, and Ray Floyd has never won the US Open. To illustrate how difficult it is to win a number of majors, only two people, Jack

Nicklaus with 18 wins and Walter Hagen with 11, have won more than ten, while Gary Player and Ben Hogan have won nine each. Tom Watson has won eight, including the Open five times and Arnold Palmer, Bobby Jones, Harry Vardon, Gene Sarazen and Sam Snead have won seven each. Nick Faldo and Lee Trevino have each won six; in Faldo's case, three Masters and three Opens. If one were asked to name, at random, the greatest golfers who ever lived, this would be a fairly universal list to which most people would add J. H. Taylor and "Young" Tom Morris. Of the contemporary golfers who have won two or more titles, Nicklaus, Watson, Floyd, Crenshaw and Ballesteros are now virtually at the end of their careers. Faldo might still add another title to his six, as might Nick Price who has won three majors, the Open and the USPGA twice. John Daly, winner of the USPGA title in 1991 and the Open in 1995, definitely has the potential to add more titles, as he, more than any other player, has the capacity to reduce a course to its knees. Greg Norman should have won more majors than he has. It is doubtful whether the day of Strange, Lyle or Langer will come again and, apart from them, no other golfer playing has won more than one major. Indeed, several have the reputation of the finest golfer never to have won a major and Colin Montgomerie is rapidly reaching the top of this list.

Clockwise from top left: "J.H." Taylor, from his portrait in Westward Ho! clubhouse, Nick Price and Greg Norman.

THE OPEN

The first Open was played at Prestwick in 1860 when it was won by Willie Park. He won the title three more times, in 1863, 1866 and 1875. The early years of the championship were dominated by "Old" Tom Morris and "Young" Tom Morris, father and son, who won the title eight times in its first 12 years. After the reign of the Morrises, Jamie Anderson and Bob Ferguson each won the title three years in succession between 1877 and 1882. They were succeeded by the "Great Triumvirate" of Vardon, Taylor and Braid who between them won the title 16 times between 1884 and 1914. The first foreign winner was Arnaud Massy of France who won in 1907 and the first American winner was Jock Hutchison who won at St Andrews in 1921. There have only been three amateur winners, John Ball in 1890, Harold Hilton in 1892 and

Top left: Willie Park Snr, the first Open Champion.

Bottom left: Arnaud Massy of France, British Open Champion, 1907.

Below: Jock Hutchison, first American winner of the Open in 1921.

1897, and the great Bobby Jones who won three times, his last victory coming in his Grand Slam year of 1930. There must be long odds against another amateur winner.

After World War I the American players started to come and compete. The only British success in that period was that of Arthur Havers who won in 1923. Henry Cotton, one of the finest golfers that Britain has ever produced, won in 1934 to end a 12-year "home" famine and again at Carnoustie in 1937, beating the entire American Ryder Cup team. His final round of 71, played in a downpour, has been called one of the greatest competitive rounds ever.

After that, the Open fell into decline as the prize money was insufficient to tempt the best American professionals, and the tournament became the preserve of Bobby Locke and Peter Thomson. There were notable American winners, Sam Snead in 1946 and Ben Hogan in 1953, but the field did not include many of the best golfers in the world. That all changed when Arnold Palmer came and conquered, and then continued to come even when he no longer conquered. After 1960 the Open returned to its place as the premier tournament in the world and the list of winners since then contains all the greatest golfers who have played in the last 32 years.

Above: Jack Nicklaus after his third Open win at St Andrews in 1978.

Far left: Henry Cotton after his win at Royal St George's in 1934.

Left: Tony Lema celebrating his victory at St Andrews, in 1964.

THE US OPEN

The first US Open was played at Newport, Rhode Island in 1895. It was won by H. J. Rawlins. Winners in the early years of the championship included Willie Anderson, who won four times between 1901 and 1905, and is the only person ever to have won the tournament on three successive occasions. John McDermott was the first "home-grown" American to win in 1911. Before that, all the winners had been expatriate Scots who made their living teaching golf in the USA. McDermott's back-to-back victories were followed by the sensational triumph of Francis Ouimet whose victory over Ted Ray and Harry Vardon in a play-off in 1913 did so much to popularize golf in the USA.

The US Open is a difficult tournament to win. Apart from Anderson, the only players to have won the title on four occasions have been Bobby Jones, Jack Nicklaus and Ben Hogan while Jones, Snead, Palmer and Nicklaus have all been second four times.

Left: Francis Ouimet, the first US captain of the R & A, from his portrait in the clubhouse.

Below: Ralph Guldahl, winner of the US Open in 1937 and 1938, drives while Ben Hogan watches.

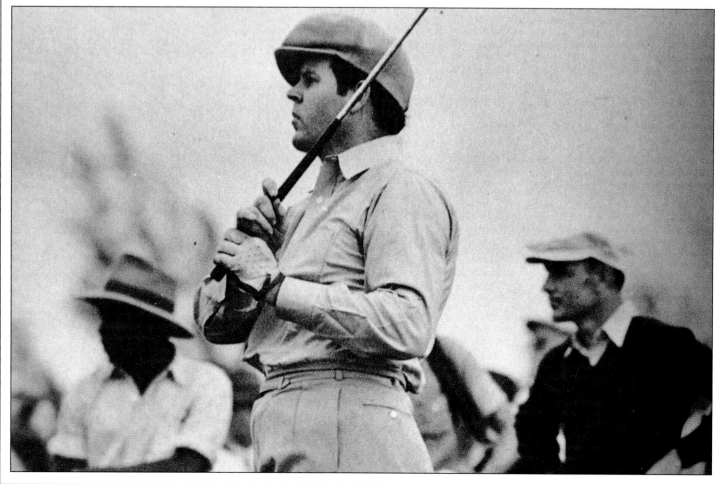

Bobby Jones, in 1929 and 1930, Ralph Guhldahl, 1937 and 1938, Ben Hogan, 1950 and 1951, and Curtis Strange, 1988 and 1989, have all won two years in succession. There have been five amateur winners: Bobby Jones, Francis Ouimet, Chick Evans, Jerome Travers and Johnny Goodman and Jack Nicklaus finished second as an amateur to Arnold Palmer in 1960.

In the last 20 years, apart from Curtis Strange, only Andy North has won the title twice and he has won only three tournaments in all on the USPGA circuit.

The tournament is almost always won by an American. Harry Vardon in 1900, Ted Ray in 1920 and Tony Jacklin in 1970, have been the only British winners, though Faldo lost a play-off with Curtis Strange in 1988 and was third in 1990 and fourth in 1992, and Colin Montgomerie also lost a play-off in 1994 and was third in 1992. The South Africans, Gary Player and Ernie Els, won in 1965 and 1994 respectively, and David Graham has been the sole Australian winner, in 1981.

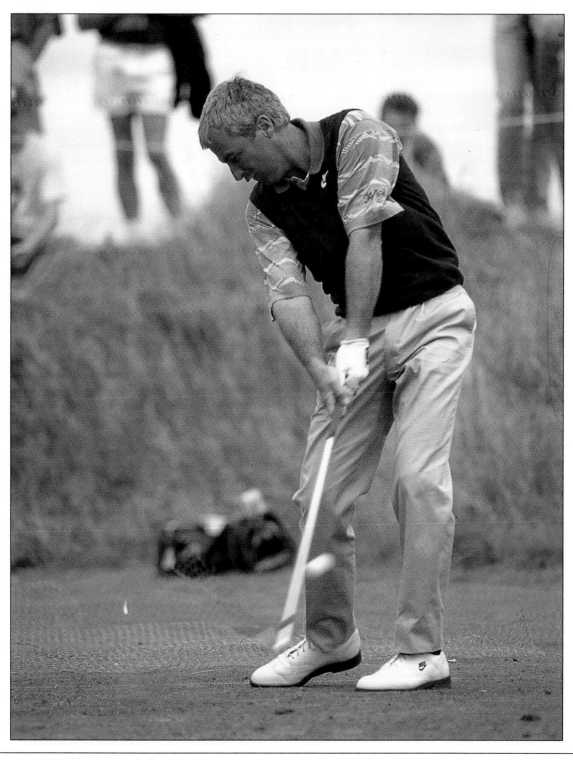

Curtis Strange, the first winner of the US Open in successive years (1988 and 1989) since Ben Hogan's back-to-back wins in 1950 and 1951.

THE MASTERS

The Masters was the creation of Bobby Jones, who designed his course at Augusta in Georgia with Dr Alister Mackenzie in the 1920s. He had the idea of inviting the leading players in the world to compete on his course each year and thus the Masters tournament was born. It is the only major tournament that is always played on the same course each year. With the rise of television, the astonishing beauty of the course and the drama that the tournament so often creates has made the Masters a worldwide favourite. Bobby Jones came out of retirement to compete in the first Masters in 1934. However, there was no fairy-tale ending and he finished 13th behind Horton Smith. Smith won again two years later and in the intervening year Gene Sarazen won for the first and only time when he holed his second shot at the par-5 15th for an albatross or double eagle – one of the most famous shots ever played on a golf course.

The first person to win the Masters three times was Jimmy Demaret, who won in 1940, 1947 and 1950. When he won in 1950 he came from five strokes behind with six holes to play. Sam Snead won the first of his three

Above: Billy Joe Patton, Ben Hogan, Bobby Jones and Sam Snead after the Masters in 1954. Hogan and Snead tied and Snead won the play-off.

Dr Alister Mackenzie helped Bobby Jones to design the course at Augusta in the 1920s.

titles in 1949 and for the next four years swopped the title with Ben Hogan. Palmer won the first of his four titles in 1958, Jack Nicklaus became the youngest winner in 1963 at the age of twenty-three, and Gary Player became the first non-American winner when he won the first of his three titles in 1961. The most prolific winner is Jack Nicklaus who has won the Masters six times. The last occasion was in 1986 when he was forty-six and so became the oldest man to win the title. By then he was no longer the youngest winner as Severiano Ballesteros won the first of his two titles in 1980 when he had just turned twenty-three, two months younger than Nicklaus had been in 1963. Seve was the first European winner and he won a second title in 1983, to be followed by the fine German golfer, Bernhard Langer in 1985. The 1987 Masters was won by Larry Mize's chip-in in a play-off to deny Greg Norman victory, and then followed four years of winners from Britain. Sandy Lyle won in 1988, playing the most miraculous shot to get down in two from a bunker 140 yards (128m) short of the pin at the 72nd hole to win by a stroke from Mark Calcavecchia. Nick Faldo won in 1989 and 1990 and became only the second person in golfing history to win back-to-back titles, Jack Nicklaus being the first in 1965 and 1966. Ian Woosnam won his only major in 1991 in another dramatic finish. Fred Couples won for the USA in 1992 to interrupt the European sequence, but Langer won for the second time in 1993 and Jose-Maria Olazabal of Spain won in 1994. Ben Crenshaw won an emotional second title shortly after the death of his guide and mentor, Harvey Pennick, in 1995. Finally,

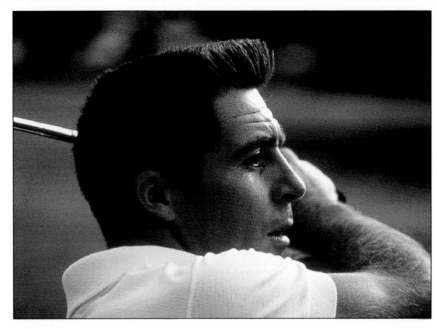

in 1996 Greg Norman looked to have spread-eagled the field at the start of the last round when he held a six-stroke lead over second-placed Nick Faldo. Norman's golf for the first three rounds, which included a record-equalling 63, had been unsurpassed. What followed was one of the most extraordinary turnarounds in golfing history. Faldo, playing with icy composure, produced a round of flawless golf while Norman simply fell apart, finishing with a 78 to Faldo's 67, the lowest round of the day. Faldo had won by five strokes. The huge crowd appeared numbed by what they were seeing; an awed hush hung over the whole course and the last holes were played in almost complete silence.

Gary Player of South Africa, the first non-American winner of the Masters in 1961. He is one of the four players who have won all four majors.

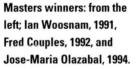

Masters winners: from the left; Ian Woosnam, 1991, Fred Couples, 1992, and Jose-Maria Olazabal, 1994.

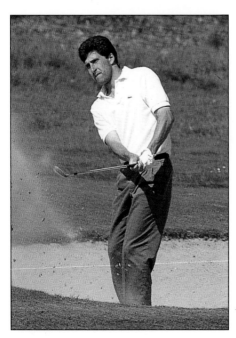

THE USPGA CHAMPIONSHIP

The USPGA Championship was first played in 1916, the year that the US Professional Golf Association was founded. It was originally a match-play event and the first winner was "Long" Jim Barnes, the Cornishman who had emigrated to the USA from England. Barnes also won the Open in 1925 and the US Open in 1921, and won the second PGA championship in 1919 after a gap of two years due to World War I. The early years of the event were dominated by Walter Hagen who won the title five times, four in succession from 1924. Gene Sarazen also won twice, beating Hagen at the 2nd extra hole in the final of 1923.

Thereafter the tournament was always won by American professionals and while the

John Daly plays out of a bunker on the way to his sensational victory at Crooked Stick, Indiana in 1991.

winners often included the great names of American golf, such as Byron Nelson, Sam Snead and Ben Hogan, there were many champions who were less well known. In 1958 the tournament changed from match-play to stroke-play and went abroad, so to speak, for the first time, when the great Gary Player won in 1962. Player won again in 1972. Jack Nicklaus is the most prolific winner in the years since the tournament became stroke-play, winning five times in 1963, 1971, 1973, 1975 and 1980. He has also been runner-up four times. Greg Norman's dismal luck in the major championships continued in 1986 with a titanic struggle with Bob Tway. The players were level as they came to the 72nd hole, Norman reached the green in regulation

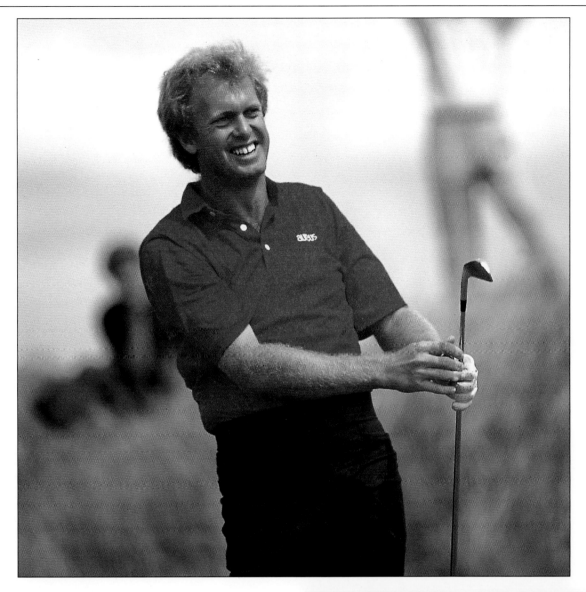

Left: Wayne Grady, the Australian winner at Shoal Creek, Alabama in 1990. He was the first non-American to win the competition since Gary Player in 1972.

Below: Colin Montgomerie of Scotland who lost a play-off for the USPGA title in 1995 to Steve Elkington.

figures while Tway found a bunker but holed his bunker shot for a birdie and victory.

Recently, the tournament captured the public imagination as never before when John Daly won at Crooked Stick in 1991. Daly was the eighth reserve to play in the event and knew he was playing only the night before the event started. His mammoth, uninhibited hitting was phenomenal and he went on to win the Open at St Andrews in 1995. In the last five years the American stranglehold on this event has somewhat diminished. Wayne Grady, an Australian, won in 1990. Nick Price, the great player from Zimbabwe, won in 1992 and 1994 while Paul Azinger won in 1993, a most popular victory for the fine player who had so nearly won the Open in 1987 at Muirfield. Steve Elkington, another Australian who plays regularly on the US tour won in 1995, defeating Scotland's Colin Montgomerie in a play-off.

THE INTERNATIONAL TEAM TOURNAMENTS

There are four major international team tournaments: the Ryder Cup, the Walker Cup, the Curtis Cup and the Solheim Cup.

THE RYDER CUP

The premier international competition is the Ryder Cup, which is played every two years between the professionals of the USA and Europe. The first two unofficial matches, between the USA and Great Britain and Ireland only, were played in 1921 and 1926 at Gleneagles and Wentworth, with Great Britain and Ireland winning comfortably. After the second match, the Ryder Cup was presented by Sam Ryder, a golfing enthusiast from St Albans, England, and a friend of the "Great Triumvirate", Taylor, Braid and Vardon. The cup was to be played for every two years on a home-and-away basis. It is believed that Abe Mitchell, another fine professional of his day, suggested to Sam Ryder that the competition become a regular event. Mitchell's statue is on top of the trophy.

The Ryder Cup was first played for in 1927 when the Americans won on home soil at Worcester, Massachusetts, by 9½ points to 2½. For many years it was dominated by the Americans, who won seven successive matches from 1935 before losing to Dai Rees' team at Lindrick in 1957. There was a dramatic tied match at Royal Birkdale in 1969 but apart from that the US domination of the event was such that it dropped out of favour and started to lose popular support.

All that changed in 1979 when it was decided that the Great Britain and Ireland team should also include the leading European players. The tournament is now played between the USA and Europe, and has produced a series of thrilling encounters, with the first US defeat for 28 years in 1985, a tied match in 1989, a one-point victory for the USA in 1991 and a one-point victory for Europe in 1995. It is contested with a ferocity that belies the belief that professionals play only for money, and competition for places in the team dominates the professional tours.

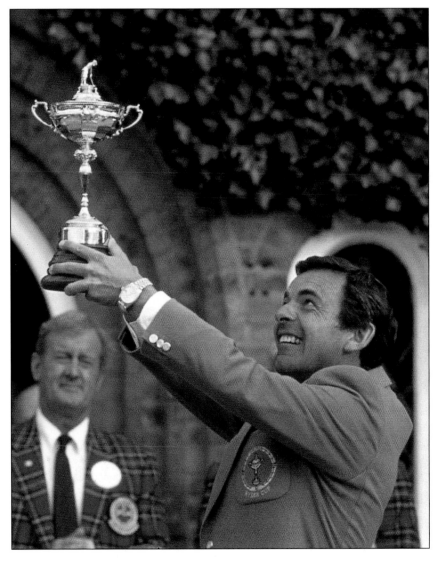

Triumph for Europe; Tony Jacklin, the winning captain, holds the trophy aloft at The Belfry, 1985.

Above: Paul Azinger, a consistent winner for America in Ryder Cup matches.

Right: Ray Floyd, US Ryder Cup captain in 1989, drives at The Belfry, 1993.

Above: Tony Jacklin and Jack Nicklaus, the two captains, at Muirfield Village, Ohio, 1991.

Left: Colin Montgomerie drives at The Belfry, 1993. He was unbeaten in his three matches.

THE WALKER CUP

Like the Ryder Cup, the Walker Cup started as an unofficial match between the best amateurs in the USA and Britain. It is five years older than the Ryder Cup. The original idea of George H. Walker, President of the United States Golfing Association, was to have an amateur competition open to all countries. The response he got was disappointing but he persevered and a team was sent from the USA to play at Hoylake in 1921. This first match was dubbed the "Walker Cup" by the local press and the Americans won 9–3. The match was played annually for the first three years but thereafter every other year. The first 31 matches, up until 1987, were generally very one-sided. The Great Britain and Ireland team won only twice, both times at St Andrews, in 1938 and 1971, and there was a tied match at 12 points each in Baltimore in 1965. Since 1989 the matches have been much more even with each country winning twice. The British victory in 1989 was the first-ever on American soil. A number of the leading professional players have played in the Walker Cup as amateurs, such as Sandy Lyle, Peter Oosterhuis and Colin Montgomerie for Great Britain, and Jack Nicklaus, Tom Kite, Gene Littler, Craig Stadler and Curtis Strange for the USA.

The first British Walker Cup team sails for America in 1922. Bernard Darwin, the great golfing writer, is on the left in the back row.

THE CURTIS CUP

The first matches between the leading amateur ladies from the USA and Great Britain were unofficial and began in 1905. In 1932 the Curtis sisters, Margaret and Harriot, both former US amateur champions, presented a cup to be played for every other year in the same way as the Walker Cup. The results of this competition have not been quite so one-sided as the Walker Cup, but there have been long periods of American domination. The third match, in 1936, was tied but the first-ever British success did not come until 1956 at Prince's, Sandwich, though in fairness there was a ten-year gap in the competition between 1938 and 1948. The 1958 match was also tied but the Americans held sway until 1986 at Prairie Dunes when the British team won for the first time on American soil. They repeated their victory two years later at Royal St George's. The Americans had their revenge in 1990 but the British won again in 1992. The match in 1994 was a nail-biting tie and the 1996 match at Killarney was again won by the British team.

Harriot and Margaret Curtis, the sisters who gave their name to the Curtis Cup.

THE SOLHEIM CUP

In 1990 the Solheim Cup was inaugurated for the leading professional women golfers in Europe and the USA, and was first played for at Lake Nona, Florida. All the ties so far have been "home wins" and therefore the Americans have two victories to the European women's one.

Kersten Solheim, who started the biennial competition.

THE EISENHOWER TROPHY

The Eisenhower Trophy, named after the American president, Dwight D. Eisenhower, is played biennially between amateur teams of four. It was first played for in 1958 and the USA has won it ten times. Other winners have been Great Britain and Ireland (three times), Australia (twice), Japan, Canada, Sweden and New Zealand.

THE WORLD CUP

The World Cup started as the Canada Cup and is played for by teams of two players from each country. There is also a prize for the lowest individual score. The competition started in 1953 and was first won by Argentina, represented by Antonio Cerda and Roberto de Vicenzo, who so unluckily lost the Masters in 1968 by signing for a 66 when he had taken 65. Thereafter, it has been won more often than not by the USA which has won it 21 times in all, including four times running from 1992 to 1995 when represented by Fred Couples and Davis Love III. Other winners include Taiwan, Sweden, South Africa, Canada, Germany, Ireland and Wales. It has never been won by England or Scotland.

Roberto de Vicenzo, winner of the first World Cup.

CHAPTER 4

THE GREAT COURSES

● ●

This is a selection which includes some of the most famous and several superb courses, but it does not claim to be a comprehensive collection. There are many courses not included here which are worth mentioning. We have tried, however, to span the world, and highlight the truly international appeal of the game.

Turnberry, Scotland, looking across the Firth of Clyde to the Isle of Arran.

Baltrusol, Springfield, New Jersey.

ST ANDREWS OLD
ST ANDREWS, FIFE

The Old Course of St Andrews, where golf has been played since 1552 and possibly earlier, is the most famous golf course in the world and yet many of the famous golfers who later sing its praises have been reluctant to admire it at first sight. The great Bobby Jones wrote that when he first played at St Andrews he felt only a puzzled dislike, but nine years later he said that if he had to select one course on which to play the match of his life it would be St Andrews. The most famous hole is the 17th, the "Road Hole", which has seen the downfall of many a would-be champion, while the 13th has been called the greatest single hole in golf. It takes time to appreciate the subtleties of the Old Course, but a round there is played in the company of the spirits of the golfing immortals.

The Royal & Ancient clubhouse, St Andrews.

MUIRFIELD
GULLANE, EAST LOTHIAN

Muirfield is a private course and belongs to the Honourable Company of Edinburgh Golfers who moved there from neighbouring Musselburgh in 1891. The original course was designed by "Old" Tom Morris. In 1892 it was used for the Open Championship but was widely criticized because it was bounded by stone walls, and was considered an inland course. It is a long course, nearly 7,000 yards (6,400m) and is renowned for the severity of its rough. Henry Cotton won the Open here in 1948, Jack Nicklaus in 1966 (he named his course in Ohio, Muirfield Village in its honour), and Nick Faldo won in the Muirfield centenary year of 1982. However, the best-known Open at Muirfield was the one that was about to be won by Tony Jacklin in 1972 when Lee Trevino chipped in at the 71st hole to snatch victory by two shots.

The 8th hole at Muirfield. This picture, showing the stone walls, was taken in 1896.

ROYAL TROON
PRESTWICK, AYRSHIRE

Troon lies next-door to Prestwick on the west coast of Scotland in the county of Ayrshire. Prestwick is the more historic course for it was there that the Open was held for the first 12 years of its existence (thereafter operating in a rota with St Andrews and Musselburgh), but Troon is longer and more demanding. The Open was first held here in 1923 and again in 1950, 1962, 1973, 1982 and 1989. Arnold Palmer won in 1962 with a masterly exhibition of golf in dry and difficult conditions. The course is most famous for the "Postage Stamp" hole, the 8th, where in one Open an unfortunate German amateur took 15 strokes.

The 8th hole at Troon.

TURNBERRY AILSA
TURNBERRY, AYRSHIRE

The Ailsa course at Turnberry has not hosted as many major championships as the other British championship courses, but it is a spectacular, much-photographed course which is a pleasure to play on.

It was remodelled after the war by Mackenzie Ross, the great golf-course architect, and the 9th hole, where the golfer drives across the sea to the fairway, is the epitome of seaside golf at its most terrifying. It was here that Watson and Nicklaus staged an epic encounter at the 1977 Open. Locked in head-to-head combat on the last day, they went round respectively in 65 and 66 with Watson winning by one shot. They finished ten strokes ahead of the third-placed Hubert Green who was the only other player in the field to beat par. It was, without a doubt, the greatest contest for the famous old claret jug. Greg Norman won the Open when it was staged here in 1986. For visitors, the second course, the Arran, is less demanding.

The famous hotel at Turnberry is built on a ridge between the two courses.

ROYAL DORNOCH
DORNOCH, SUTHERLAND

It has been said many times that Dornoch would have hosted the Open were it not so inaccessible. It was the home of Donald Ross, the great American golf-course architect, and its influence is found in courses throughout the USA. It is a wonderful seaside links with natural plateau greens and the 5th, 14th and 17th are all particularly admired. The earliest mention of golf being played at Dornoch is in an account from 1616.

Royal Dornoch on a fine day in early summer. The picture shows the step in the 8th fairway.

GLENEAGLES KING'S COURSE
AUCHTERARDER, PERTHSHIRE

● ●

Gleneagles is a magnificent golfing experience. It is situated in the middle of Scotland with the Ochil Hills to the south and the Highland mass of the Grampians to the north. The setting is spectacular and it has been said that on a fine morning in autumn there is no more beautiful place to play golf in the world. There are four courses, all linked to the Gleneagles Hotel, of which the King's and Queen's courses, originally designed by James Braid (the five-times Open champion), are the best known.

Right: Gleneagles Hotel, Perthshire, Scotland.

Below: The 12th hole on the King's course at Gleneagles.

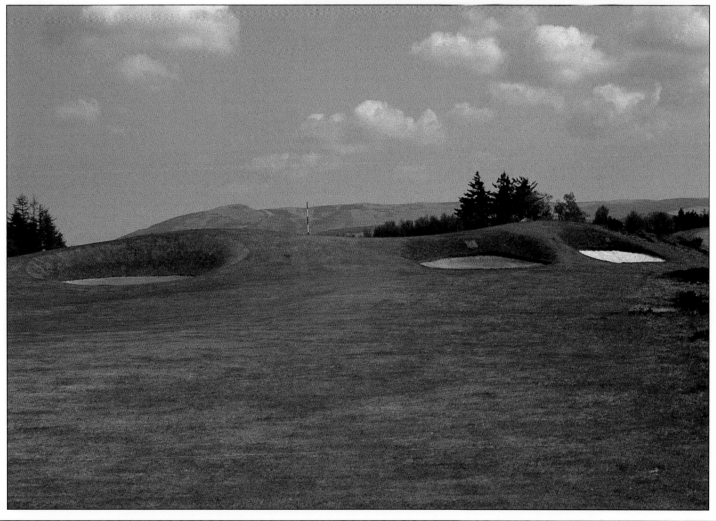

NORTH BERWICK
EAST LOTHIAN

• •

North Berwick has never hosted the Open but it is a historic course, part of that great stretch of golfing country along the south coast of the Firth of Forth. It is famous for several of its holes: the 2nd, the "Sea Hole", where even the slightest touch of a slice puts you on the beach; the 14th, "Perfection", where the second shot is played blind over a large hill to a pole with the green almost in the sea; and the 15th, the "Redan", one of the most copied short holes in the world.

> A North Berwick caddie was carrying the bags for a young professional in his first tournament when they came to the 18th tee. He pulled the driver out of the bag.
> "I don't need the driver here, I'll go over the green if I hit it," said the young professional.
> "You'll no hit it," was the reply.

The 3rd green at North Berwick with the Firth of Forth in the background.

PRESTWICK
AYRSHIRE

• •

No book on golf should fail to mention Prestwick, where the first Open was played and which was the home of that championship for the first 12 years of its existence. In 1873 the Open moved to St Andrews for the first time and Prestwick then fell into a rota with St Andrews and Musselburgh until 1894 when the Open was first held on English soil at Royal St George's. Prestwick is now too short for championship golf and it is too cramped to handle the vast crowds that attend the major championships, but there are few more demanding courses, especially when the wind is blowing. The course is most famous for the 3rd hole, the "Cardinal", a par-5 guarded by the great Cardinal bunker, the 5th, the "Himalayas", a blind par-3 over a range of sand dunes, and the 17th, where the second shot is again blind over the "Alps" to a small green guarded by a famous sleepered bunker.

The 4th green with the "Himalayas" beyond at Prestwick.

ENGLAND

ROYAL BIRKDALE
SOUTHPORT, LANCASHIRE

R oyal Birkdale is probably the finest of the championship courses that run along the Fylde coast north from Liverpool as far as Royal Lytham and St Annes just south of Blackpool. It is noted for its 5, 4, 5, 4 finish. The Open was first held here in 1954 and was won by the great Australian golfer Peter Thomson, and again in 1961, when Arnold Palmer won. Palmer's victory was marked by an astonishing recovery shot from the rough at the 15th (now the 16th) when, from behind a bush, he hit the ball to within 15 feet (4.5m) of the pin. (A plaque near the bush commemorates this feat.) Lee Trevino won here in 1971, Johnny Miller in 1976, when Severiano Ballesteros was second. Tom Watson won his only Open on English soil here in 1983 and Ian Baker-Finch won in 1991.

Above: The 16th hole, where a plaque commemorates Arnold Palmer's great shot.

Left: The 5th at Royal Birkdale. The course was summed up by Peter Thomson as "man-sized, but not a monster."

ROYAL LYTHAM AND ST ANNES
LYTHAM ST ANNES, LANCASHIRE

A justly famous links course that was laid out in 1897 and first held the Open in 1926 – the year the course was granted "Royal" status. The Open has been held at Royal Lytham nine times and surprisingly enough there had never been a professional American winner until 1996, when Tom Lehman won the title with a record low score for the course. The great Bobby Jones won the second of his British Grand Slam titles here in 1926. It was at the 17th that Jones played a miraculous shot from scrub on the right of the fairway to within feet of the pin. The shot destroyed the hopes of Al Watrous who, when he saw it, said, "There goes $100,000". Bobby Locke of South Africa won here in 1952, Peter

Thomson in 1958, Bob Charles from New Zealand in 1963, and Tony Jacklin became the first British player to win for 18 years in 1969. The other winners were Gary Player in 1974 and Severiano Ballesteros in 1979 and 1988.

"Golf at Lytham", 1904.

ROYAL ST GEORGE'S
SANDWICH, KENT

The best-known course in the south of England, Royal St George's was once more host to the Open Championship in 1981, when it was won by Bill Rogers. Sandy Lyle won here in 1985. The Open was also held here in 1993 when Greg Norman won with the lowest score ever recorded in the Open, 267, which gave lie to the claim that St George's was the most difficult of all the Open courses. There has been a slight sense of anti-climax over the Opens held here since the

War. It was at Royal St George's that Henry Cotton went round in 65 in the second round of the 1934 Open, which was commemorated by Dunlop with the Dunlop 65 ball. Tony Jacklin also accomplished the first televised hole-in-one at the short 16th.

An aerial view of Royal St George's.

Harry Bradshaw, leading the field at the Open at Royal St George's in 1949, found his ball lying in a broken beer bottle at the back of the 5th green. He elected to play it and, although he smashed the ball out of the bottle, he took a 6. This misfortune meant that he tied the tournament with Bobby Locke and then lost the play-off.

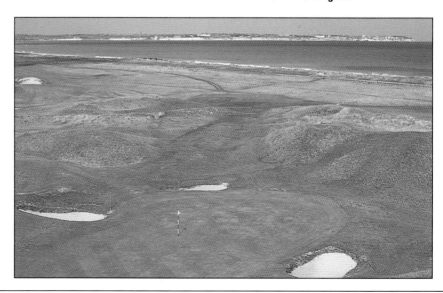

WENTWORTH
VIRGINIA WATER, SURREY

Wentworth is not a links course and therefore the Open Championship is not played there, but it is certainly the best-known inland course in England and plays host each year to the World Matchplay Championship and the Volvo PGA Championship. It is known as "The Burma Road" because of its length and the course ends in two par-5 holes of which the 17th measures 571 yards (522m). It was opened in 1924 and has been the scene of many memorable encounters. Arnold Palmer won the first World Matchplay event in 1964, Gary Player won five times in the next nine years, Severiano Ballesteros has also won the event five times and Sandy Lyle has reached the final five times but has won only once. The South African, Ernie Els, won the event for two years running in 1994 and 1995.

Above: The clubhouse at Wentworth.

Below: Waiting to play: the approach to the 7th green at Wentworth.

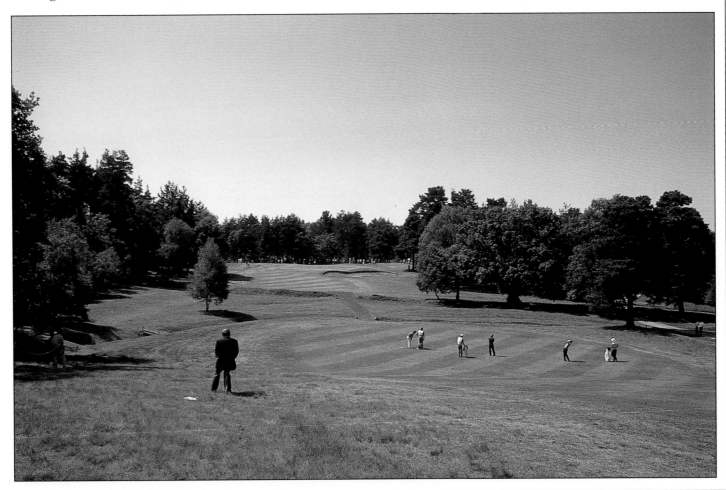

AMERICA

AUGUSTA
GEORGIA

● ●

Augusta was the result of a suggestion made by a New York banker, Clifford Roberts, to the great Bobby Jones. The course was laid out by Alister Mackenzie in the 1920s in the grounds of a disused nursery. Viewers of the Masters on television will have seen the spectacular flowering shrubs that line the fairways and which give each hole its name. Augusta is the most exacting course and yet built with such subtlety that the average player can play round quite happily. The Masters tournament, which is held there each spring, produces spectacular golf when the greens, specially prepared, are lightning fast and to score well the professional has to put his approach shot in exactly the right place. The course is best known for the 11th, 12th and 13th holes, which were named the "Amen Corner" by the American golfing writer, Herbert Warren Wind, who recommended a quiet word with the Almighty as an aid to playing them without disaster.

Above: The 16th green at Augusta during the Masters championship.

Left: Dr Alister Mackenzie, the designer of Augusta, wearing the Mackenzie tartan.

PEBBLE BEACH
CALIFORNIA

O ne of the best-known courses in the USA, Pebble Beach was created by S. F. Morse with the help of the golf-course architect Jack Neville. It contains a number of spectacular holes, such as the par-5 6th with its green perched on the headland, the par-3 7th where the green points out into the ocean, and the 8th where the Pacific has to be carried with the second shot. Jack Nicklaus twice landed on the beach in the US Open of 1972. Tom Watson birdied the last two holes, considered to be two of the toughest closing holes in golf, to win the US Open by a stroke from Jack Nicklaus in 1982. The major championships are not held there as often as they might be because the course lies 120 miles south of San Francisco and is thought to be a bit too far from any major city.

The 8th hole at Pebble Beach.

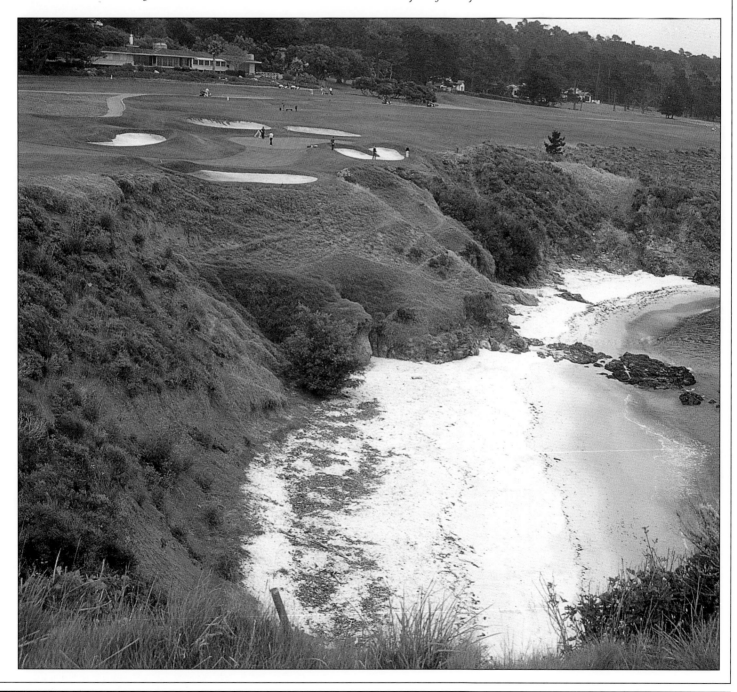

CYPRESS POINT
PEBBLE BEACH, CALIFORNIA

One of the two great courses on the Monterey Peninsula (the other is Pebble Beach), Cypress Point was designed by Alister Mackenzie who used the natural surroundings to the full to construct a magical course bounded by the Pacific Ocean. The most famous hole is the 16th, a par 3 of 233 yards (214m) across the ocean, which is where many balls end up; only the best shots get home. This is followed by the 17th, another spectacular dog-leg hole across the Pacific Ocean. The course is not really long enough to be used for the major championships and the club is very exclusive.

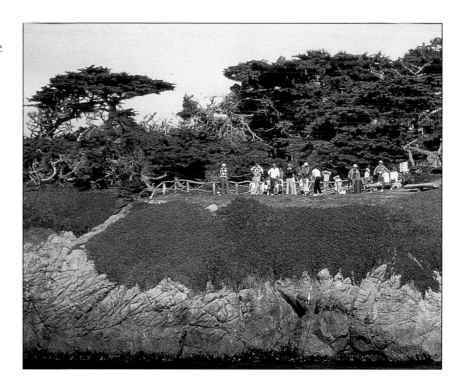

The 11th tee at Cypress Point.

BALTUSROL
SPRINGFIELD, NEW JERSEY

Baltusrol has staged the US Open a record six times and the event has been played on three different courses. The original course, constructed in 1895, was of nine holes only. In 1920 A.W. Tillinghast was appointed to redesign the course and he constructed two 18-hole courses, the Upper and the Lower. The US Open was played on the Lower course in 1954, 1967 and 1980 while the Upper course hosted the 1936 Championship. Jack Nicklaus won the last two US Opens held at Baltusrol. He beat Arnold Palmer in 1967 with a last round of 65 to Palmer's 69 to win by four strokes, but he eclipsed that record in 1980 when he played the 72 holes in 272 strokes, which was not equalled until 1993 by Lee Janzen. Baltusrol is a long course at over 7,100 yards (6,500m) with a championship par of 73. Baltusrol's best-known hole is probably the short 4th, which plays across a lake to a green guarded by a wall, and it has the longest 17th and 18th holes in championship golf.

An aerial view of the 18th, 4th and 3rd holes at Baltusrol.

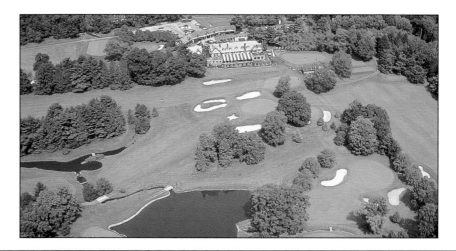

MERION
ARDMORE, PHILADELPHIA

The 10th hole at Merion.

Below: Hugh Wilson, the amateur golf-course architect who designed Merion in 1912.

Merion is probably the most fascinating golf course in the USA. The US Open has been held here four times, though not since 1981, when it was won by the Australian David Graham. Perhaps its lack of length is finally telling against it in this age of boron-shafted clubs and "Big Bertha" drivers. Merion was designed by an amateur, Hugh Wilson, who was an expatriate Scot, and first opened for play in 1912. The original Merion Club was a cricket club and the club name was not changed to Golf until 1942, although, by then, golf had long been its main activity. The course contains a number of great holes. The 1st is a savage dog-leg to the right with the green heavily defended by bunkers. The 8th, though only 360 yards (330m) long, has a most teasing drive and a second shot onto a tiny plateau green totally surrounded by bunkers. The 11th is the hole where Bobby Jones won the last of his Grand Slam titles in 1930 by 8 and 7. It has a tiny pear-shaped

green guarded by bunkers on the left and Cobb's Creek running round the front of the green to the rear. Gene Sarazen took seven shots at this hole and lost the 1934 US Open by one shot because of it. The 18th hole is one of golf's great finishing holes and the finest shot played to it was Ben Hogan's 1-iron in the 1950 US Open which finished inches from the pin and enabled him to tie with Lloyd Mangrum and George Fazio. He won the play-off by four shots from Mangrum.

OAKMONT
PENNSYLVANIA

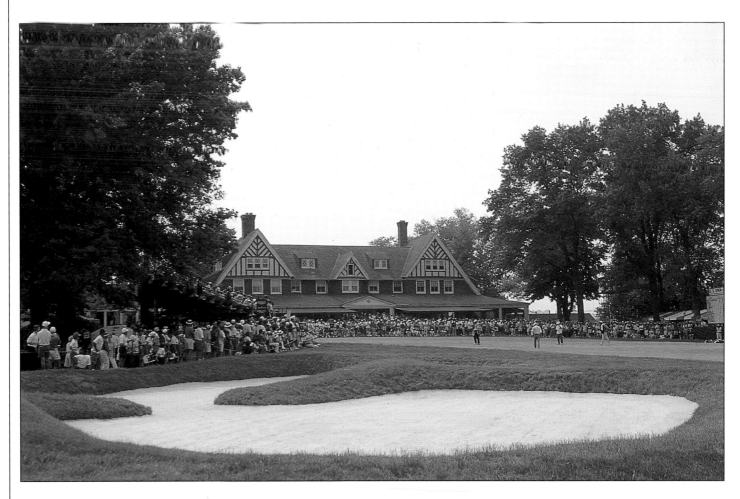

The Oakmont Country Club was created by Henry C. Fownes, a Pittsburgh industrialist who set out to build the toughest golf course possible. Although Oakmont has been made easier, between the wars there were over 350 bunkers, raked with a special furrow rake so that the wayward shot exacted an inevitable penalty. Fownes, so it is said, used to walk round the course noting those shots that were less than perfect and if they did not land in a bunker would order another to be constructed. The greens were shaved to a height of under an eighth of an inch and were terrifyingly fast. Jimmy Thomson remarked in the 1935 US Open that he had marked his ball with a dime and the dime had slid off the green. As a result, when the US Open was first played at Oakmont the course even defeated the great Bobby Jones, who

finished well behind Tommy Armour who won with a total of 301 after a play-off with H. Cooper. In 1935 the US Open returned to Oakmont and was won by Sam Parks, who broke 300 by one shot. Ben Hogan won there in 1953 with a score of 283, which was equalled by two of the all-time greats, Arnold Palmer and Jack Nicklaus, in 1962. Nicklaus won the play-off. Johnny Miller won in 1973 when, after rain, he shot a 63 in the final round to come from six behind to win. Larry Nelson did much the same in 1983 with final rounds of 65 and 67 to beat Tom Watson by one shot. The best-known hazards are the "Church Pews" bunker, with its seven grass ridges lying between the 3rd and 4th fairways, and the "Sahara" bunker, which guards the left side of the 8th green and is 120 yards (110m) long by 30 yards (27m) wide.

The 18th green at Oakmont in 1994 during the US Open which was won by Ernie Els after a play-off.

OAKLAND HILLS
BIRMINGHAM, MICHIGAN

This was the course dubbed "the monster" by Ben Hogan after his win there in the US Open of 1951. He added, "If I had to play that course every week, I'd get into another business". Originally, the course had been set out in 1917 by Donald Ross, the golf course architect from Dornoch who had such an impact on American golf-course design at the beginning of the twentieth century. However, Ross's course was felt to be too easy for the modern professional and was remodelled by Robert Trent Jones for the 1951 US Open. Jones narrowed the landing areas of the drives and added bunkers that most players had difficulty carrying from the tees; he also allowed the rough to grow in. Many players did not like his alterations, especially when Ben Hogan, then at the height of his powers, opened with a 76. However, Hogan followed this with rounds of 73, 71 and 67 to win from Clayton Heafner, with Bobby Locke and Jimmy Demaret down the field. His last round is considered to be one of the greatest ever played. The course, at nearly 7,000 yards (6,400m), has a championship par of 70 with as tough a finishing stretch as any other course in the world. The best championship score was the 272 made by David Graham when he won the USPGA Championship there in 1979 after a play-off. The unknown Steve Jones won with a total of 278 in 1996, beating Davis Love III and Tom Lehman by one shot in a gripping finish. He became the first prequalifier to have won the US Open since Jerry Pate in 1976.

Above: Robert Trent Jones, one of America's greatest golf-course architects.

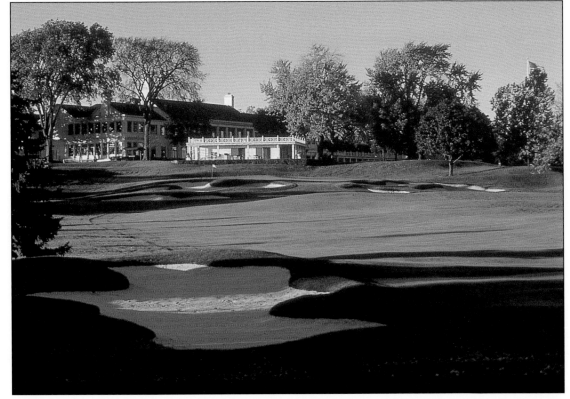

Looking up the 18th fairway to the green and clubhouse at Oakland Hills.

SHINNECOCK HILLS
SOUTHAMPTON, NEW YORK

Shinnecock Hills was the first 18-hole golf course to be opened in the USA and the club was one of the five founder members of the USGA. It was originally designed by a Scot, Willie Dunn Jnr, in 1891. While on holiday at Biarritz, France, William K. Vanderbilt had seen Dunn play and he brought him to Long Island to lay out a course on a site that had originally been a burial ground for the Shinnecock tribe of North American Indians. Dunn's course was originally 12 holes but it was extended to 18 in 1893 and redesigned by Dick Wilson in 1931 when it became obvious that the course was too short for championship golf. The US Open had first been held at Shinnecock in 1896 but it was not until 1986 that it returned, when the title was won by Ray Floyd with a total of 279, only one stroke under par. In 1995 Corey Pavin celebrated the Shinnecock centenary by winning the third US Open to be held there with a level par score of 280. The short 7th hole is named after the "Redan" at North Berwick and the 17th, the "Eden", is named after the estuary which surrounds the famous Old Course at St Andrews.

The final green at Shinnecock Hills in 1995, when the US Open was won by Corey Pavin.

WINGED FOOT
MAMARONECK, NEW YORK

One of the hardest of all the championship golf courses, Winged Foot was designed by A.W. Tillinghast for the members of the New York Athletic Club who said they wanted a "man-sized course". They may have got more than they bargained for. The course has a championship par of 70 with only two par-5 holes. The difficulty of the course lies in the par 4s: there are ten over 400 yards (365m) and when you add to that the closely guarded slick greens and severe rough when the course has been prepared for a championship, it is little wonder that the course has been so difficult to conquer. The US Open has been held here four times. In 1929 Bobby Jones won in a play-off with Al Espinoza after he had thrown away a huge lead over the last nine holes. In 1959 Billy Casper won with a magical display of putting: he took 114 putts in all, single-putting 31 greens, and ended up with a score of two over par! In 1974 Hale Irwin won the first of his three US Open titles with a total of 287, seven shots over par. Finally, in 1984 there was a titanic clash between Fuzzy Zoeller and Greg Norman who tied after 72 holes. Norman had holed a putt of 40 feet (12m) to birdie the 72nd hole and draw level but, unfortunately for him, the play off was one-sided and Zoeller won easily.

A.W. Tillinghast, designer of Winged Foot.

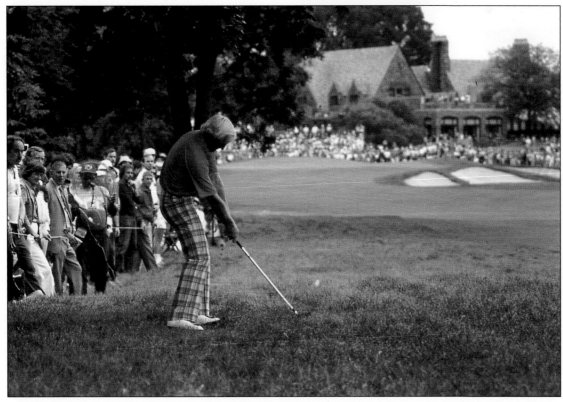

Greg Norman playing at Winged Foot in 1984, when he tied with Fuzzy Zoeller.

AROUND EUROPE

PORTMARNOCK
COUNTY DUBLIN, REPUBLIC OF IRELAND

Portmarnock in Ireland has been acclaimed as one of the most beautiful places to play golf on a fine summer's day, surrounded as it is by water, with a view of the Mountains of Mourne sweeping down to the sea in the distance. And yet when the wind blows the course can become as tough and demanding as any seaside links. The course was founded by two local men, W.C. Pickeman and George Ross, who rowed across the estuary to make a golf course. Pickeman and Mungo Park, the 1874 Open Champion, made the first course in 1894 and it was extended by Fred W. Hawtree in the 1970s. The two finest holes are the 14th which, though only 385 yards (352m), is played out towards the sea to a plateau green surrounded by bunkers and slopes. This is followed by the short 15th which Arnold Palmer called the best short hole in the world.

Portmarnock has played host to many championships, including the Dunlop Masters, the Canada Cup (now the World Cup), the Carroll's Irish Open and the British Amateur Championship. The most memorable day in the history of the course was at the Irish Open Championship in 1927 when all the tents were blown out to sea and only one player, George Duncan, broke 80 in the afternoon to win by a shot from the great Henry Cotton, who had consecutive rounds of 86 and 81. In contrast, when the weather is benign, the Irish rain has fallen to soften the greens and the winds are light and balmy, the course offers little defence to the best modern professionals. Bernhard Langer's highest round in the 1987 Carroll's Irish Open was 68 and he beat par by no fewer than 19 shots.

Criticism comes in all shapes and sizes. Ted Ray, winner of the Open in 1912 and the US Open in 1920, was asked by a persistent club member to share with him the secret of his great length from the tee. "Hit it a bloody sight harder," was the down-to-earth reply.

Portmarnock on a fine day looking out to sea.

EL SALER
VALENCIA, SPAIN

This course was designed by Javier Arana, who is responsible for many of the best new courses in Spain – particularly the Club de Campo outside Madrid. El Saler is considered his finest course. It lies close to the Mediterranean and contains a fascinating mix of inland and sea-side vegetation. The sand dunes that lie alongside the 7th, 8th, 17th and 18th holes are very like the best links courses in Britain and the fairways are flanked by lovely umbrella pines. Bernhard Langer won the Spanish Open here in 1984 with a last round of 62.

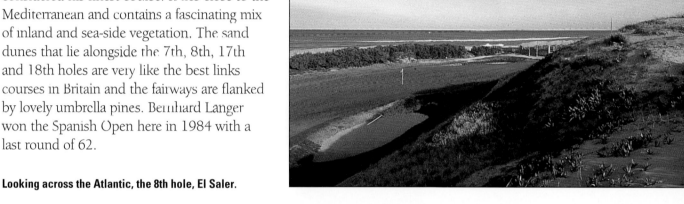

Looking across the Atlantic, the 8th hole, El Saler.

VALDERRAMA
SOTOGRANDE, CADIZ, SPAIN

Valderrama was laid out by Robert Trent Jones in 1964 when it was known as Los Aves. He revised his design in 1985, when the course was renamed, with the object of making it one of the finest championship courses in the world – a Spanish Augusta. The course is now acknowledged as being extremely difficult and the back nine is among the hardest in the world where, rather than birdies, pars are the goals. It is extremely picturesque and the beautiful scenery with the old cork trees, which occur as natural hazards at some holes, may prove a distraction. It was the home of the Volvo Masters before this tournament moved to Wentworth and is due to host the Ryder Cup in 1997.

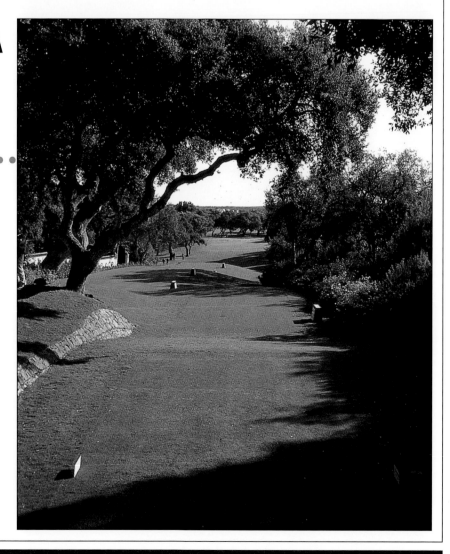

The old cork trees which shade the 18th tee are one of the most striking features of Valderrama.

PENINA
PORTIMÃO, ALGARVE, PORTUGAL

Penina is synonymous with the late Sir Henry Cotton, the great British golfer of the 1930s and 1940s, who made his home here when he retired from competitive play. The course was built on flat land transformed by the planting of thousands of trees and shrubs. Now that these are mature, the course is a demanding test for the best players and enormously long from the back tees. The back nine starts and finishes with two par 5s. Every shot has to be carefully planned. The PGA sponsors promising young professionals to attend the school there each autumn.

The complex at Penina was the inspiration of Sir Henry Cotton, who started his golf school here.

CRANS-SUR-SIERRE
MONTANA, SWITZERLAND

The course at Crans-sur-Sierre, 5,000 feet (1,524m) above the Rhône valley in the Alps, was originally laid out in 1904 by Sir Arnold Lunn, the founder of modern skiing. The present course was opened in 1927 and the Swiss Open has been held here every year since 1939. The course is not particularly long and in the high atmosphere the ball flies huge distances. In 1978 Jose-Maria Olazabal shot a European 9-hole record of 27. The backdrop of the Matterhorn makes the course immensely spectacular.

Sir Arnold Lunn, better known as a pioneer of Alpine skiing, designed Crans-sur-Sierre. The Alps make a spectacular backdrop and the ball can be hit huge distances in the thin mountain air.

ST-NOM-LA-BRETÊCHE
VERSAILLES, PARIS, FRANCE

St-Nom-la-Bretêche course was designed by Fred Hawtree and is one of the most popular in France. It is situated just outside Versailles near Paris and has hosted the Lâncome Trophy for many years. It was the scene of the World Cup in 1963 when it was won for the USA by Arnold Palmer and Jack Nicklaus, a pretty powerful combination. It has also held the French Open on a number of occasions.

When he was a young player Bobby Jones was a great talker on the course. Playing with Harry Vardon in the US Open of 1920, Jones played a bad pitch shot which ran through the green.

"Did you ever see a worse shot than that, Harry?" he asked.

"No," replied Vardon.

The round was finished in silence.

St-Nom-la-Bretêche is a fine parkland course. Nick Faldo is on the left of the picture.

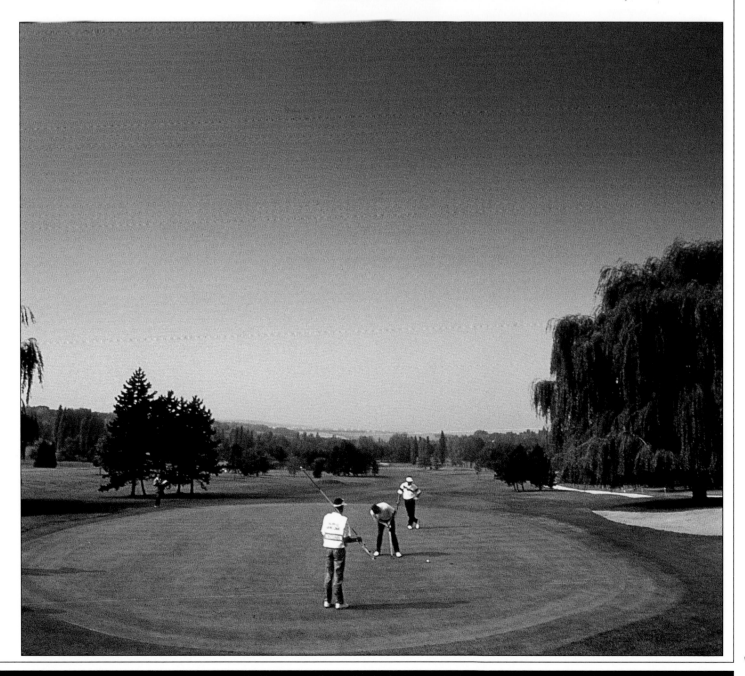

REST OF THE WORLD

ROYAL MELBOURNE
BLACK ROCK, VICTORIA, AUSTRALIA

The championship course at Royal Melbourne is a composite of the East Course, designed by Alex Russell in 1932, and the West Course, designed by Dr Alister Mackenzie. It was first used for the Canada Cup (the World Cup) in 1959. The club was founded in 1891 and the West Course was laid out by Mackenzie in 1924 – a number of the holes are reminiscent of Augusta. The finishing hole is one of the most demanding par 4s in world golf. The 6th and 14th holes are testing dog-legs which punish anything but the most accurate of club selection. Perhaps the best-known feature of the course is its always lightning-fast greens.

The composite course at Royal Melbourne which is used for championships.

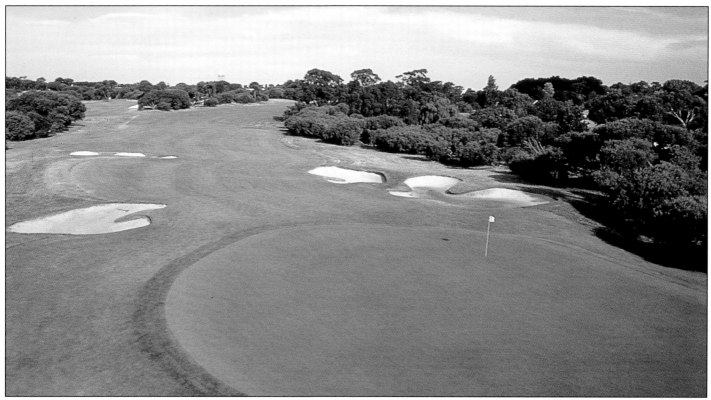

ROYAL SYDNEY
ROSE BAY, NEW SOUTH WALES, AUSTRALIA

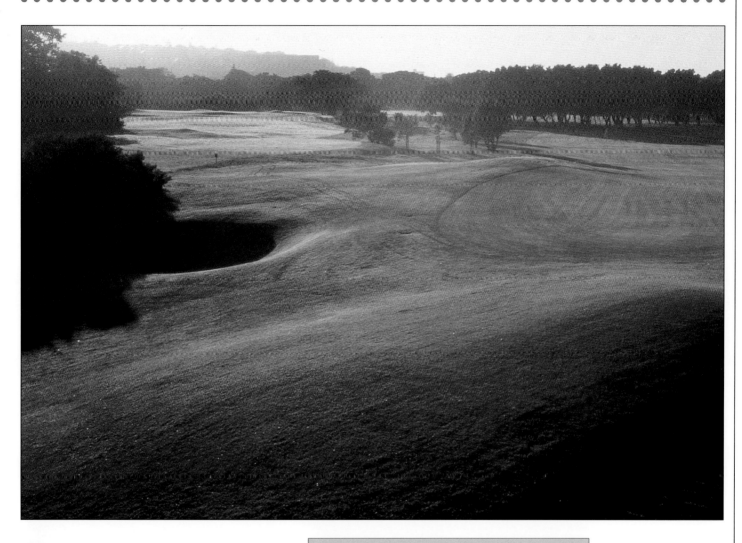

Above: Royal Sydney's 18th hole at sunrise.

The Royal Sydney Golf Club was founded in 1893 and the course was remodelled by Dr Alister Mackenzie in the l920s. It is one of the finest courses in Australia, close to the sea but only ten minutes away from the centre of Sydney. The best-known holes are the 18th – a dog-leg to the left of 410 yards – and the short 3rd, surrounded by bunkers filled with dazzling soft, white sand. The main features of the course are the undulating fairways, fearsome rough and the gleaming white sand of the bunkers.

About the putter there is something so slender and sensitive, so fitful, capricious and fickle, shall I venture to say even at times inconstant, that no doubt can be felt as to the sex question. Plainly, such a companion will not readily be chanced on among the common herd or met with in the crowded streets; she must be sought for with care and skill. No club is so human as the putter, none so worthy the name friend, if true, none more likely to do one an injury if disloyal and treacherous. Like so many of her sex, the putter has a touch of vanity in her nature which must be humoured, if she is to be won as a faithful mistress. (John J. Low)

ROYAL CALCUTTA
TOLLYGUNGE, CALCUTTA, INDIA

The Royal Calcutta Golf club was founded in 1829 and deserves a mention here due to its being the oldest golf club in the world outside Great Britain.

Royal Calcutta was granted its royal status by King George V in 1911 and is maintained to the highest standards. It is very long, nearly 7,200 yards (6,580m) from the back tees and has a mass of water hazards. The course may appear easy at first sight but it is not and the par-4s require particularly accurate iron play from the fairways while the greens are full of subtle undulations. Another hazard used to be kraits, small but deadly snakes, which were sometimes found on the fairways. The course was originally in the Dum-Dum area of Calcutta, which is where the international airport is now, and it moved from there to Tollygunge where the course was developed from a paddy field. The whole course is only a few feet above River Ganges. The Indian Amateur Championship, one of the oldest championships in the world, has been held on the course since 1892.

JAPANESE COURSES
FUJIYAMA, MOUNT FUJI, JAPAN

Golf is enormously popular in Japan, where it has become a status symbol with the membership of the top clubs costing hundreds of thousands of yen. The terrain is not generally suited to the construction of golf courses but the Japanese have solved the problem by cutting the tops off mountains and filling in the valleys to create fairways. The first course in Japan at Kobe, which was created by Arthur Groom in 1903, was built in this way and many others followed. A number of the leading golf-course architects have worked in Japan, among them Pete Dye, who laid out the course at Mariya in 1987. This is one of the most testing courses in Japan with many water hazards and an island green on the short 17th. It is set in lovely rolling country and the immaculately maintained fairways are surrounded by pine forests which give the course a great feeling of tranquillity and calm. Other good Japanese courses include Yomiuri, Fujiyama, which lies at the feet of Mount Fuji and Gotemba.

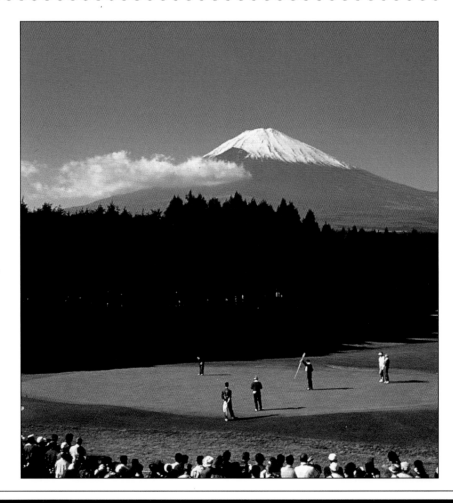

Fujiyama, in the shadow of Mount Fuji.

THE GARY PLAYER COUNTRY CLUB
SUN CITY, PILANESBERG, NORTH-WEST PROVINCE, SOUTH AFRICA

Sun City is an interesting course laid out by Gary Player and Ronald Kirby on the floor of an extinct volcano. The course was cut from thorn scrub and bush and is best known for promoting the $1,000,000 challenge which, when it started, was the richest tournament in the world. Nowadays, as prizes have grown higher, the tournament has lost some of its interest. The course is very long and for championship play can be stretched to 7,650 yards (7,000 m).

The million-dollar challenge of 1994 is watched by a large crowd at Sun City.

EMIRATES
DUBAI, UNITED ARAB REPUBLIC

The Dubai Desert Classic is now held annually on the Emirates course, which was designed and laid out by Karl Litten. It is one of the early events of the European tour. The course is watered by a lavish sprinkler system with 500 sprinkler heads spraying nearly a million gallons of water on the course every twenty-four hours. The course is a triumph of man over nature and the classic is now a much-respected event. Fred Couples won there in 1995 and Colin Montgomerie won in 1996 with a sensational shot from the fairway with his driver to birdie the 72nd hole.

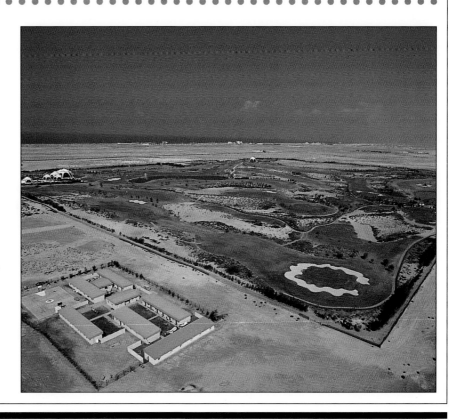

The Emirates club, looking parched in spite of the massive amount of water it receives.

23.—A DUFFER'S STROKE.

7.—MISSED THE GLOBE.

41.—THE BRASSEY.

18.—"DELIGHTS OF A BUNKER."

5.—AN ENTHUSIAST.

30.—NEW WOMAN.

33.—MACFOOZLE.
Chief of the Clan.

35.—A NOVICE.

3.—KEEP YOUR EYE
ON THE BALL.

10.—A BAD LIE.

50.—LOST BALL.
One of our poor relations.

40.—THE GRACES OF
GOLF.

CHAPTER 5

COLLECTABLES AND MEMORABILIA

T hrough the years, many pieces of golfing memorabilia have been produced to commemorate tournaments or celebrate the game and its players. Collecting these pieces is almost a sport in itself for some people, and there are some fascinating artefacts to be found.

A collection of 50 cigarette cards was produced by Cope's tobacco of Liverpool.

Various golfing memorabilia, including a feathery and a fine long-nosed wood.

GOLFING ARTEFACTS

The most obvious and well-known golfing memorabilia must be cigarette cards, hoarded, swapped and treasured by school children and adults alike in their day. These continue to be among the most evocative pieces of golfing history, with their cartoon pictures and humorous captions. Other items might be part of a limited-edition ornament, produced to commemorate a specific event, and redolent of the period in which it was made.

A statue of Arthur Balfour, a keen golfer as well as a British prime minister.

An original cut-glass vinaigrette with silver golf clubs – the perfect gift for a salad-loving golfer!

A traditional Doulton cream jug, with a less traditional golfing scene painted on it.

The distinctive British Open medal of 1887.

Various items from a collection of golfing memorabilia.

A golfing plate: "The Nineteenth Hole".

A US Open Championship medal.

INDEX

Augusta 76

Ballesteros, Severiano 48
Baltusrol 78
Braid, James 40

Cotton, Henry 42
Crans-sur-Sierre 86
Curtis Cup, The 64
Cypress Point 78

Eisenhower Trophy, The 65
El Saler 85
Emirates 91

Faldo, Nick 48

Gary Player Country Club, The 91
Gleneagles King's Course 71
Golf, 1890-1945 24
Golf, The End of the Nineteenth
    Century 16
Golf, The Palmer Years 30
Golf, The Post-war Years 28
Great Triumvirate, The 40

Hagen, Walter 41
Hogan, Ben 43

International Team Tournaments, The 62

Jacklin, Tony 47
Japanese Courses 90
Jones, Bobby 41

Langer, Bernhard 49
Locke, Bobby 44

Masters, The 58
Merion 79
Morris, "Old" Tom 38
Morris, "Young" Tom 39
Muirfield 69

Nicklaus, Jack 46
Norman, Greg 49
North Berwick 72

Oakland Hills 81
Oakmont 80
Open, The 54

Palmer, Arnold 45
Park Junior, Willie 39
Pebble Beach 77
Penina 86
Player, Gary 45
Portmarnock 84
Prestwick 72

Robertson, Allan 38

Royal Birkdale 73
Royal Calcutta 90
Royal Dornoch 70
Royal Lytham and St Annes 74
Royal Melbourne 88
Royal St George's 74
Royal Sydney 89
Royal Troon 69
Ryder Cup, The 62

Sarazen, Gene 42
Shinnecock Hills 82
Snead, Sam 43
Solheim Cup, The 65
St Andrews Old 68
St-Nom-la-Bretêche 87

Taylor, John 40
Thomson, Peter 44
Trevino, Lee 46
Turnberry Ailsa 70

US Open, The 56
USPGA Championship, The 60
Valderrama 85
Vardon, Harry 40

Walker Cup, The 64
Watson, Tom 47
Wentworth 75
Winged Foot 83
Women in Golf 32
World Cup, The 65